LANDSCAPING
IDEAS THAT WORK

LANDSCAPING
IDEAS THAT WORK

JULIE MOIR MESSERVY

The Taunton Press

The Taunton Press
Inspiration for hands-on living®

The Taunton Press, Inc.,
63 South Main Street, PO Box 5506
Newtown, CT 06470-5506
e-mail: tp@taunton.com

Editor: Christina Glennon
Copy editor: Katy Zirwes Scott
Indexer: Jim Curtis
Interior design: Carol Petro
Layout: Bethany Gracia
Illustrator: Bethany Gracia
Cover photographers: (Front cover, top, left to right): Allan Mandell, Ken Gutmaker, Mark Lohman, Susan Teare;
Bottom: Paul Wieczoreck/Champlain Valley Landscaping; (Back cover, clockwise from top right): Brian Vanden Brink,
Susan Teare (2), Mark Lohman (3)

The following names/manufacturers appearing in *Landscaping Ideas that Work* are trademarks: Acrylite®, Corten®,
Gunite®, Pinterest®

Library of Congress Cataloging-in-Publication Data
Messervy, Julie Moir.
  Landscaping ideas that work / author: Julie Moir Messervy.
    p. cm.
  Includes index.
  ISBN 978-1-60085-780-5
1. Landscape design. 2. Landscape gardening. I. Title.
  SB473.M4463 2013
  635.9--dc23
                              2013029350

Printed in the United States of America
10 9 8 7 6 5 4 3 2

ACKNOWLEDGMENTS

This is my third book with The Taunton Press. Both *Outside the Not So Big House* and *Home Outside: Creating the Landscape You Love* were so well received that I kept asking to do more! It turned out that Taunton's popular Ideas That Work series was lacking a book about landscape design, so here it is at last. Series editor Carolyn Mandarano was a delight to partner with; her flexibility in trusting my design studio, JMMDS, with so many of the tasks that go into creating an elegant book is appreciated. Book editor Christina Glennon smoothed the prose and tightened the ideas. Lynne Phillips oversaw the book's layout and design, while photo editor Erin Giunta coordinated the work with a host of superb landscape and architectural photographers. Special thanks go to Laurie Black, Todd Caverly, Jim Fiora, Tria Giovan, Ken Gutmaker, Chipper Hatter, Mark Lohman, Allan Mandell, Eric Roth, Bill Sumner, Susan Teare, Brian Vanden Brink, Virginia Weiler, and Lee Ann White.

A great debt of gratitude goes to the landscape professionals and the homeowners who answered the call for submissions and took the time to send us such wonderful projects. While each designer cannot be directly credited in our captions, the book could not have been written without their generous contributions. Please refer to the back of the book for specific crediting.

This book was a delight to write because of JMMDS's talented staff—there's just nothing that they cannot take on. Bethany Gracia, our wonderful landscape and graphic designer, laid out and illustrated the book with her always-elegant hand; Jennifer Silver ably helped write and direct the details into place; landscape architect Erica Bowman helped write the plantings chapter; and landscape architects Jana Bryan and Anna Johansen read through the final manuscript, improving and perfecting it. Please check out our online landscape design service at www.homeoutsidedesign.com and also our iPhone/iPad app, Home Outside Palette. And for more of our designs, books, lectures, and even a little philosophy, go to www.jmmds.com. We'd love to hear from you!

CONTENTS

Introduction   2

CHAPTER 1

Designing Your Landscape   4

Get Started 6

Create a Wish List 16

PUTTING IT ALL TOGETHER
DIY Backyard 18

CHAPTER 2

Spaces That Work   20

Making Space 22

Front Yards 24

PUTTING IT ALL TOGETHER
Formal Front Yard 26

PUTTING IT ALL TOGETHER
Romantic Front Garden 31

Side Yards 32

Backyards 36

Driveways and Garages 44

PUTTING IT ALL TOGETHER
A Charming Garage 46

CHAPTER 3

Open-Air Rooms   50

Getting Some Air 52

Porches 54

Decks 58

PUTTING IT ALL TOGETHER
An Updated Arbor 60

Patios 62

PUTTING IT ALL TOGETHER
Outdoor Living at Its Best 64

THE ESSENTIALS
Paving Options 66

Lawns 68

Pools 70

Sheds and Outbuildings 74

Shade Structures 76

PUTTING IT ALL TOGETHER
East Meets West 78

CHAPTER 4

Walls, Fences, and Hedges   80

Enclosures 82

Walls 84

PUTTING IT ALL TOGETHER
A Green Wall 88

PUTTING IT ALL TOGETHER
Terracing down the Slope 94

THE ESSENTIALS
Wall Materials 96

Fences 98

Hedges 102

Gateways 104

Railings 106

Edging 108

THE ESSENTIALS
Finished Edges 110

CHAPTER 5

Paths and Walkways 112

Path and Passage 114

PUTTING IT ALL TOGETHER
Colorful Crossroads 120

THE ESSENTIALS
Path Materials 126

Steps and Stairs 128

Bridges 132

CHAPTER 6

Plantings 134

Planting Schemes............. 136

Bed Layouts 138

PUTTING IT ALL TOGETHER
Rain Garden 140

Trees 142

PUTTING IT ALL TOGETHER
Inside a Tropical Retreat 148

Shrubs...................... 152

Climbers 154

Perennials 156

PUTTING IT ALL TOGETHER
An Abundant Garden 158

Grasses 160

PUTTING IT ALL TOGETHER
Grassy Xeriscape 162

Ground Covers 164

Annuals 168

Containers 170

Edibles 174

PUTTING IT ALL TOGETHER
Pack 'Em In 176

Greenhouses................. 178

CHAPTER 7

Details in the Landscape 180

Delighting in the Details 182

Focal Points................. 184

PUTTING IT ALL TOGETHER
Water Music 192

PUTTING IT ALL TOGETHER
Gather around the Fire 196

Furniture 200

PUTTING IT ALL TOGETHER
Light and Lively 204

Lighting 208

PUTTING IT ALL TOGETHER
A Complete Courtyard 212

Credits 214

Index 217

INTRODUCTION

In this age of digital devices and screens, our need for time and space in the out-of-doors is essential to our physical, mental, and even spiritual health. One way to engage with nature is to create a landscape around your house that draws you and your loved ones outside. If you build it, they will come—to bask with a cup of coffee in the early morning rays, to play hopscotch on the driveway, to harvest the ripest tomato along with a snip of basil for a fresh caprese salad, to plant a rose bush, or to catch fireflies in the grassy meadow under the stars. These real-life experiences bring to children and adults alike a deep connection to our earth and a rekindling of spirit that can't happen any other way.

And guess what—it's just not that hard to create a landscape that works. In the pages of this book, you'll find a host of visual ideas, as well as design tips, before and after images, case studies, and essential information that will get you started. I walk you through the process we use at JMMDS, my landscape architecture and design firm, from documenting your site and figuring out your aesthetic preferences to thinking about your property from big picture all the way down to the details. The goal is to create comfortable living spaces in the out-of-doors and we—and the other design professionals featured in this book—know how to help. You'll find a range of projects, from luxurious spaces to those that were built with sweat equity on a shoestring. What's common to each is the quality of their designs. Be inspired!

DESIGNING

We all want a landscape that works well with

our particular site, dreams, and way of life.

YOUR

With just a little planning, your home outside

is within reach.

LANDSCAPE

Get Started

Congratulations! You are the proud owner of a piece of property. If you're like many people, you feel pretty comfortable choosing paint colors for the walls and carpeting for the floors, but when you walk outside, you freeze. Without four walls, a floor, and a ceiling, you haven't the first idea of where to begin.

It can be both daunting and discouraging to try to figure out how to make landscape improvements to your property without the help of a professional designer. If you've bought a new home, the contractors probably left you with a completed house on an unfinished site; if you own an older landscape, you have to deal with someone else's taste. How do you figure out what to do? How do you even begin?

You break it down into parts. Start by understanding your property, including issues of location, sun and shade, soils, slope, and planting zone. Then look closely at your house—its size, style, layout, and inside/outside relationship. Next, think about yourself and your family—your style, your temperament, and your needs for your property—what do you want to have happen there?

Every site is different and each person is unique. This means that you need to do some research to better understand your property, and a bit of soul-searching to figure out your particular personality, background, style, and needs. Let's get started.

top right • When you move into a new home, there's a lot to think about when dealing with the land around your house. Even though this is an older home, it still sits on an empty landscape, ripe for a new, more personal design.

bottom right • You can take cues from your house's materials and style. This home's stucco walls extend into the landscape, giving structure to the outdoor rooms while melding house and garden.

Making the home outside as comfortable as the home inside takes some understanding of yourself and your site. This homeowner created an open-air room that works, complete with a four-poster bed under the stars!

YOUR PROPERTY

Where you dwell—in the country, the city, or the suburbs—can affect the way you are able to live on your land. In the city, you would be very lucky to own outdoor space of your own, whether it's a roof deck, a garden, or a balcony. Instead, you may rely upon public open space like parks or community gardens to act as substitutes for your own backyard. Houses in suburban neighborhoods are often built around the needs of families, complete with private backyard spaces, driveways, and garages, with easy walking access to community amenities. Country properties might be larger in scale, with vast vistas and views, or set in a village where homes are nestled near a market, a school, and a church. In every case, your land is a precious commodity, so understanding its opportunities and constraints is critical to designing the landscape around your house.

Whether you live on a level piece of land or one that slopes will affect what you can do there. Land that slopes away from your house is desirable because it drains water away and enables long views out. Land that slopes toward your house can bring drainage headaches—a good perimeter drain helps—but enables you to look right into the upward-facing slope. When thoughtfully planted, a hillside view that can be readily seen from inside the house can almost literally bring the outside in, no matter the weather.

Once you have a good plan to work from (see "Sharpen Your Pencil" on the facing page), you can start to note the site conditions like sun and shade, topography, soils, drainage, and wind. The amount of sun and shade your property receives throughout

above • A house made from an old barn perches at the edge of a simple promontory of land, a grand playground to suit an active family's needs. Tough but beautiful plantings along the slope keep the bank from eroding.

above • For urban dwellers, a rooftop offers both prospect and refuge, if designed right. This lucky owner got both by creating corners to nestle against in this large open aerie.

Sharpen Your Pencil

Whether you are starting in a new home or you want to make some changes to your existing landscape, testing out your ideas on paper is the best way to begin.

DRAWING A PLAN

- Start with accurate measurements of your house. If you don't have an architect's drawing, walk around outside, using a long tape measure to mark the location of doors, windows, steps, water spigots, etc.; the more detailed you get, the more information you will have to plan your landscape. You can label the first floor rooms (kitchen, dining room, etc.) to keep in mind important views and entries.

- Measure the distance from your house to survey pins, to locate your house in the right place within your property. It's a good idea to include a north arrow to remember where the sun is (and isn't).

- Locate your driveway, paths, planting beds, trees, and other outdoor features. To locate single or freestanding objects, take measurements from two corners of your home. (Sometimes noting the width or height of objects is helpful. How tall is the large shade tree and how far will it cast its shade? How wide is the canopy of its leaves?)

- Transfer all of these measurements onto graph paper; allow each square to represent a certain length, like 2 feet or 5 feet. Choose a scale that works best for your property.

- Make note of the pluses and minuses of your yard—which views you love, which views you should screen. Where is the shade in the hot afternoon? Where is the lawn most worn away from foot traffic? Think about the views from inside your home; which rooms highlight views to the yard?

- Keep these notes in a journal dedicated to ideas for your landscape. It will be easy to reference them when you come across a wonderful new plant or product at the local garden store.

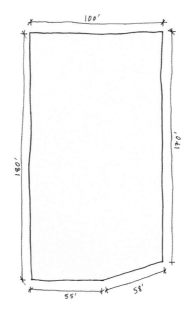

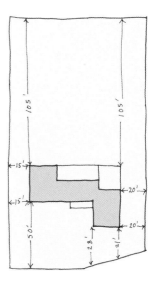

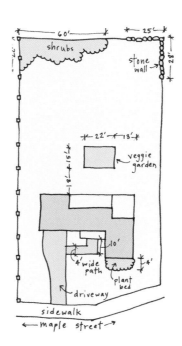

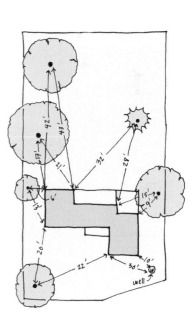

YOUR HOUSE

Your house and its style should also affect what you choose to create for the landscape around it. If you live in a Cape Cod-style cottage, for instance, you might choose to stay in that style by selecting a white picket fence, whitewashed window boxes, and hydrangea plantings, along with brick or stone walkways and terraces. If you live in a more contemporary house with flat roofs and concrete and glass walls, you may prefer a clean, spare landscape of ornamental grasses, concrete walkways, and glass railings to match the architecture.

As we'll discuss in Chapters 4 and 5, your house also provides many clues as to how best to lay out paths, patios, enclosures, and special features on your land. A formal Georgian house looks best with straight lines and symmetrical planting beds, whereas a Japanese-style home is best set off by asymmetric plantings, offset paths, and low-slung walls.

above • A historic house fits comfortably into its landscape when surrounded by a belt of old-fashioned plantings, topped by an American flag. A crunchy gravel driveway comes right up to the front door.

right · Your personal aesthetic, along with the style of your house, offers useful information about how to begin the design process. Here, daisies seeded into a wildflower meadow meld perfectly with the simplicity of this shingled Cape Cod-style house.

below · Consider the views of the garden through each of your windows—they frame a picture of your landscape. Also, what you create inside your house can relate to what's outside.

YOUR STYLE

In order to figure out what particular design style and aesthetic appeals to you, you'll need to ask yourself some questions. Are you a practical person who thinks first about the details necessary to make something work or someone who imagines first and fills in the facts later? Do you hope to share your landscape with lots of people or maintain it for your own mostly private pleasure? Do you prefer an orderly landscape with everything in its place, or are you happier with a relaxed and casual garden?

Similarly, ask yourself and your loved ones about aesthetic preferences. Do you like a landscape that is formal or informal? Do you prefer straight lines or curved ones? Would you rather have a spare, open landscape, or one that's filled with plantings? Which appeals more to you, representational or abstract sculpture? Would you rather have a landscape with dark, shady spaces or light-filled ones? Uncovering everyone's preferences is helpful as you work through any design or planning process and will help you to organize your wish list of projects.

above · This informal, eclectic landscape has a handmade quality indicative of a high level of involvement by the homeowner.

left · This concrete pathway shows a predilection for spare contemporary detailing. Cutouts filled with river stone and low ground covers bring a soft quality to a paving choice that might otherwise feel too cold and hard.

A Tropical Retreat

Tropical in Seattle? Why not? Your particular style and sensibility should help dictate what you create in your own outdoor space. Here, a simple stucco house on a busy street was turned into a private oasis by the addition of a tall bamboo fence. Elegant plantings of Hakone grass (*Hakonechloa macra* 'Aureola'), a scarlet cultivar of Crocosmia (*Crocosmia x curtonus* 'Lucifer'), and a dwarf bamboo (*Sasa veitchii*) billow out to soften lawn and sidewalk, making this tiny front yard a place we all wish we could be.

right • The original landscape did not make the most of the available space.

below • By surrounding a modest stucco house with exuberant and colorful plantings, the homeowner turned this property into a personal work of garden art.

BEFORE

Create a Wish List

Now that you understand the conditions on your property, it's time to address what you and your loved ones want to do there. Do you need recreation space for young children? Multifunctioning areas for family dinners? A firepit? A vegetable garden? A cozy corner for stringing up a hammock?

To understand better how you actually want to use your property, fill out the Using Your Home Outside questionnaire on the next page. It will give you a good sense of the atmosphere you're trying to create, the activities you want to undertake, and the features that will enhance your life in the out-of-doors. Creating a wish list of desired projects helps you envision what you hope to achieve on your land in the long term and can help you make phasing choices about each of the projects over time.

You can also create a scrapbook or Pinterest® board of ideas and images that illustrate what you're hoping to achieve. Find pictures of elements you want to add to your landscape and identify what style best suits your taste and temperament.

When you add up all the information about you and your family's lifestyle and needs, with the conditions on your site and the style of your house, you get a pretty complete picture of what you can create on your land. Next is the hard part—pulling it all together into a layout that works.

above • Some of us long for a highly planted paradise where we can take care of the birds while making a hideaway for ourselves.

right • This homeowner solved two problems at once—creating high retaining walls to hold back the sloping site while building an intimate open-air room, complete with a water feature as the focus. It's always useful to keep a wish list of the elements you'd like on your land.

Using Your Home Outside

How would you like to use your outdoor space? Defining the activities you'd like to engage in on your property will help define the design.

ATMOSPHERE

- ☐ *Hideaway*
- ☐ *Welcoming*
- ☐ *Relaxing*
- ☐ *Private*
- ☐ *Contemplative*
- ☐ *Wildlife habitat*
- ☐ _____
- ☐ _____
- ☐ _____
- ☐ _____
- ☐ _____
- ☐ _____
- ☐ _____
- ☐ _____
- ☐ _____
- ☐ _____

ACTIVITIES

- ☐ *Festive gatherings*
- ☐ *Grilling/cooking*
- ☐ *Dining*
- ☐ *Yoga/exercise*
- ☐ *Lawn games*
- ☐ *Children's play*
- ☐ *Sunbathing/stargazing*
- ☐ *Birdwatching*
- ☐ *Homesteading*
- ☐ *Gardening*
- ☐ *Animal-keeping*
- ☐ _____
- ☐ _____
- ☐ _____
- ☐ _____
- ☐ _____
- ☐ _____

FEATURES

- ☐ *Hammock*
- ☐ *Swimming pool*
- ☐ *Firepit/fireplace*
- ☐ *Hot tub*
- ☐ *Sauna*
- ☐ *Flower garden*
- ☐ *Chicken coop*
- ☐ *Vegetable garden*
- ☐ *Reading nook*
- ☐ *Potting shed*
- ☐ *Orchard*
- ☐ *Furniture*
- ☐ *Water feature*
- ☐ _____
- ☐ _____
- ☐ _____
- ☐ _____

DIY Backyard

As described by these homeowners—a young couple and their two children, ages 5 and 7—this "wide bowling alley of a yard" was featureless and uninviting. It didn't match the warmth of their home's interior, and it certainly didn't draw anyone outside. Although it is a small, narrow lot, the homeowners had an ambitious list of requests for the space: grow flowers, vegetables, and herbs; include children's play spaces and hiding places, a hammock and other spots for relaxation and reading, outdoor dining and entertaining, and sunbathing and stargazing; create privacy and screen certain views; and provide a welcoming entrance for the home office in the cottage behind the house.

The homeowners love color and whimsy and embraced the concept of open-air rooms, defined by outbuildings, fences, and planting beds. They also shared a preference for curving lines in the landscape.

JMMDS worked with them to create a plan that integrated perfectly with their needs. As soon as they received their final design, they went to work preparing the space, installing white picket fencing to delineate the garden rooms, and readying the beds for planting in the spring. To create the oval lawn at the center, they laid out a garden hose and adjusted it until the curves were just right, used orange landscape paint to mark the shape, and then cut deep edges to define the beds. Brightly colored plantings and painted outdoor furniture complete the design.

right · Sweeping curves help define the entry into the garden.

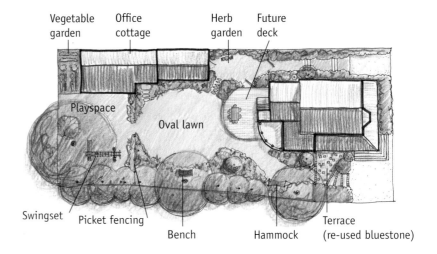

right • The backyard as it looked before. The kids help map out the new oval lawn area with a garden hose.

far right • The house as seen from the back of the property.

The garden revealed—in its first year! The lush planting beds are filled with a combination of trees, shrubs, perennials and annuals to bring color throughout the growing season.

SPACES

Breaking your property into zones

helps define the way you live on your land.

THAT WORK

Making Space

Your property, much like your house, is composed of a series of spaces that function in different ways from one another. Understanding the purpose and possibilities for each of these zones around the house helps you break down the design of your landscape so that it's not quite so overwhelming.

Like your front hall or foyer, the front yard acts as a welcoming zone and entry area into the property. Similar to your living room, den, or dining room, the backyard creates wonderful opportunities for family gathering, play, and getaway. And like a corridor or hallway in your house, a side yard offers an attractive passage that links spaces together.

Depending upon the amount of light and the topography of each, these spaces can look and feel quite different from one another. A sunny front yard will feature a very different planting palette from a shady side garden; a backyard that nestles into a planted hillside will feel far more private than a grassy front yard that opens onto the street. As always, your own aesthetic preferences should influence how each space works and feels.

top right • An easy-to-install concrete paver terrace unites garage and house as an open-air room where dining and entertaining can take place.

bottom right • Privacy is valued both inside and out. Tall curtains can be unfurled when an intimate evening outside is desired.

Which do you prefer? Geometric, curvy, or linear? These basic layouts are good starting points for making spaces that work.

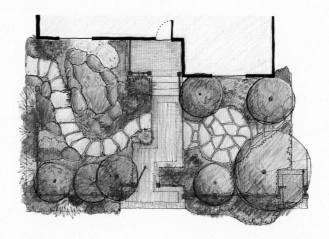

CURVY

Includes spaces that are composed of curving, rather than straight, lines. Soft arcing shapes, circles, ovals, and S-curves are appealing perhaps because they echo what we see in nature.

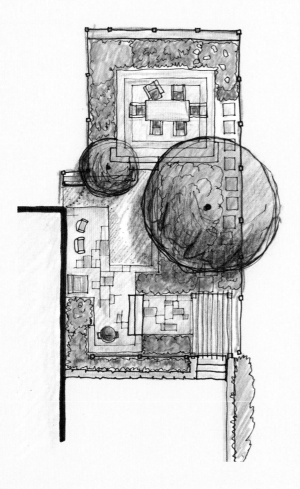

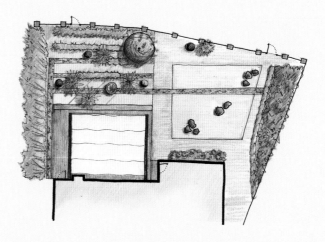

GEOMETRIC

Takes its cues from the built environment. Geometric incorporates shapes such as squares, rectangles, and even triangles. Replicating a shape or element of your house offers a satisfying way to link inside and outside.

LINEAR

Uses straight lines to organize the spaces around your house, creating a dynamic interrelationship between structure and landscape. Pergolas, paths, patios, and enclosures can be placed parallel, perpendicular, or diagonal to the plane of your house, creating energetic alignments.

Front Yards

As properties shrink in size and space is at a premium, front yards are taking on new roles to better support the life of the family. Rather than the typical broad swath of front lawn, the front yard has also become a welcoming entryway as well as a comfortable living space. No longer just made up of overgrown foundation plantings, now rain gardens, edible landscapes, and riotous perennial borders are planted in this valuable land at the front of the house.

The layout of your front yard also conveys the first impression visitors have of your home and, by extension, your personality. A lively, colorful cottage garden centered on a painted bench gives passersby a very different image of who you are than would a bland open lawn.

There are special problems and opportunities that affect the design of a front yard. When the house sits far above or below the street, getting to it requires thoughtful planning. Similarly, if a house rests too close to a street, it pays to enclose the front yard, not only for safety's sake, but to increase usability as well. Reframe your thinking: what if you treated your front yard as though it were a backyard. How would it function differently from the way it does right now?

top right · A patio beside the front door can be an unexpected and welcoming touch. Here, the herringbone brick patio, inviting chairs, and bountiful window boxes create a friendly entrance.

bottom right · This suburban home enjoyed a nice large sweep of lawn, but the homeowners decided to create a more interesting space with lots of plantings.

facing page, bottom · A stately planting of river birches, ferns, and ground cover flank a bluestone walkway, leading eye and foot up to the front door.

Edible Front Yard

At first glance, this planting looks like many other handsome front yards in this suburban neighborhood. But look more closely and you'll see a host of edibles to harvest, including kale, artichoke, and lettuce, interspersed with herbs including basil and sage. Sometimes the best sun exposure is along the street edge. Why not put it to good use while also beautifying the neighborhood?

Formal Front Yard

When you own a formal house, it can pay to extend its proportions right out to the street. This formal front yard was created to complement the designer's own foursquare 1911 Colonial home in an older neighborhood in upstate New York. The boxwood hedge parterre is laid out in an Arts and Crafts design, which echoes a stained-glass window in the house. The garden is visible from several high vantage points (front and side porches and roof garden), so its intricate design can be fully appreciated from above. The owners, landscape architects A.J. Miller and Mariane Wheatley-Miller, fill the beds with evergreens and annuals.

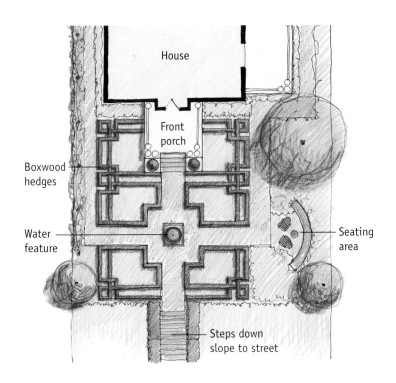

right • Far more interesting than lawn, the parterre offers lovely views from inside the house. The property sits on a natural drumlin high above the level of the street; steps lead down to the sidewalk below.

The limestone water basin occupies the perfect center of the front garden, and the sound of the fountain can be heard in an adjacent sitting area.

STEPPED FRONT YARDS

Not everyone lives on level ground. Sloping front yards and houses that sit above (or below) the street require a series of stairs or steps to reach the front door. With thoughtful design, the experience of scaling a height can be exciting rather than arduous.

Think of a series of steps and landings as being like a waterfall. The front door is the "origin" of the falls; the front stoop or porch is where it "dams up" and then flows down the steps, pooling where landings occur, until it "spills" out to meet the road or sidewalk below.

Make the steps wide enough for two people to walk side-by-side, complete with landings every few feet of rise so that visitors can catch their breath. For safety's sake, place lights so that every step is well lit. Direct water runoff into adjacent planting beds or lawn areas so that the steps remain dry.

top right • Landscape steps look and feel good when the riser is low and the tread is long. Here, two offset stairways are linked by a long level walkway before reaching the front door.

bottom right • These concrete stairs provide a handsome stepped walkway through a colorful garden. Note the location of the landings that provide visitors with a place to catch their breath every four risers.

facing page • The wooden bollards on either side of this walkway echo the roofline and bring the architecture into the garden, while also scaling down the entrance to pedestrian traffic. Billowing grasses soften the house and walkway's squares and angles. Concrete pavers and dimensional wall blocks combine to create inexpensive but handsome planters.

ENCLOSED FRONT YARDS

When you place a wall, fence, or hedge around your front yard, you turn it into something special. An enclosed space along the sidewalk provides a protected place for sitting as well as an edge against which you can plant your favorite flowers. Your front yard becomes your front garden and shows off a bit of your personal style to the world.

Surrounding the front of your property with low hedges or fencing helps keeps the world out and children in, while still allowing passersby to peek in and enjoy what they see. Such front yards present a useful alternative to traditional lawn-and-foundation planting designs, especially where space is at a premium. Why not use the front of your house for living, entertaining, and play, just as you do in the backyard, and enjoy this valuable piece of real estate?

above • This front yard sits close to the street, yet the protection of a thick stucco wall creates an enclosed space for family dining and entertaining.

left • An attractive wooden fence turns a front yard on a busy urban street into a private garden, yet the open design along the top of the fence prevents it from appearing unfriendly. A wide planting strip outside the fence means the view is as enjoyable from the street as it is from within the garden.

Romantic Front Garden

This stucco cottage would be as at home in a fairy tale as it is in a southern California beach-side community, thanks to its ivy-clad walls and cottage garden.

Romantic touches such as the picket fence and matching old-fashioned streetlamp enhance the quaint effect. The gently swooping fence is set well back from the sidewalk, creating a narrow front yard but ample space for ferns, hydrangeas, and potted plants placed where passersby can appreciate them.

Though enclosed with a low picket fence, this front yard feels open to the world. Visitors can peek in and imagine the hidden life behind the home's façade.

top right • A curving brick walkway and gate left welcomingly ajar beckon visitors toward the front door. Typical cottage garden plants of English ivy, zonal geraniums, ferns, and hydrangeas cover the landscape.

bottom right • The white chairs with their nautical blue cushions invite us to inhabit them—even if only in our minds.

Side Yards

Depending upon your property, a side yard can be a narrow sliver of space between buildings or an area wide enough to house a garage or even a terrace. In either case, a side yard can feel oddly separate from the rest of the property if its design doesn't include details—like plantings or hardscape features that are repeated in the front yard or backyard—that integrate the side yard into the entire design.

What unites most side yards is their function as passageway between front yard and backyard. It is important to design a path that flows easily between spaces. Do you want a functional walkway that serves as the shortest distance between two often-visited points? Or would you like a meandering stepping-stone path that slows you down enough to notice a lovely plant, an attractive framed view, or an interesting focal point?

Hemmed in by buildings as these spaces can be, light and air circulation are often at issue. The use of open styles of fencing, where fencing is needed, can let in more light and create a greater sense of spaciousness. Many useful and utilitarian items can be housed in a side yard, such as a tool shed, compost bin, dog run, or grill, because this space is often just out of public view.

In planning your side yard, don't forget the neighbors. If privacy is a concern, erect a high fence or tall plantings to block visual and physical access between yards. By adding a gate, you can maintain a friendly relationship between the properties.

Similar to a front yard, a roomy side yard can also function the way a backyard does: for entertaining, dining, or relaxing. And if your kitchen door opens onto your side yard, it's a wonderful place to locate a grill or pizza oven. Just make sure to include a buffet table and some comfortable chairs nearby, so the grillmeister of the family can socialize while serving up the meal.

above • A diagonal path meanders from driveway to firepit terrace, located on the side of this property. A handsome covered porch adds yet another sitting spot.

left • A narrow slit looks wider with the addition of a hydrangea hedge and tendrils of ivy that curl over a path of regularly spaced double stepping stones.

Side yard weaves into backyard on this narrow lakefront site. A large pergola brings shade to a teak dining set overlooking the water.

above • This side yard doubles as a front garden and informal entry porch. Friends and family enter this way.

right • A path of limestone pavers leads to a gate to the back forty. Shade plantings fill the beds and settle the house into this handsome side yard.

Backyards

When we want to get outside, we usually gravitate to the backyard, where all manner of outdoor living can occur. Behind our house, protected from passersby or neighbor's view, we feel the freedom to do—and be—whatever we want. The best backyards enjoy a comfortable relationship between inside and outside, visual screening from neighbors for privacy, and an interesting view or focal point, either on the property itself or beyond its bounds.

Whereas a front yard creates the first impression visitors will have of your home and should make you and your guests feel welcomed, the backyard exists to lure people outside. It should look inviting from indoors, and it could serve any number of functions (and often several at once). Your backyard might be a space for entertaining and family dining, recreation and children's play, relaxing and enjoying quiet time, hobbies such as gardening or painting, and just spending time outdoors (for all household members—human and otherwise). Even the tiniest backyard, thoughtfully designed, can accommodate most if not all of these needs for gathering, for play, and for getting away.

Unless you're lucky enough to have a large property with grand vistas, you probably will want to enclose your backyard with a fence, hedge, or wall high enough to keep prying eyes out and children (and dogs) in. At the same time, adding large windows and French doors to the back of your house encourages easy visual and physical access between inside and out.

top right · **A colorful tree bench hugs the old apple tree climbed by generations of kids.**

bottom right · **Big comfortable chairs set into a sunken terrace bring the inside out in this cozy backyard garden with an expansive view.**

A tiny backyard with a contemporary feel. Concrete and wood walls give privacy to the family when they dine outdoors.

GATHERING SPACES

Most of us long to turn our backyard into a place where family and friends love to gather, whether it be for dining out under the stars or sitting around the firepit making s'mores and conversation. All you need is a level area—paved or decked is best—that allows safe and easy passage between house and landscape and extends the floor of your house outside. Easy access to your kitchen always helps.

right • In one tiny space, this urban backyard has it all: close proximity to the kitchen, privacy from neighbors, and a beautiful focal point that draws the eye toward the middle of lush gardens.

above • Inviting chairs set around a firepit on this clean-lined terrace are an extension of the indoor living room.

In this urban courtyard corner, a sweet seating area is nestled under the umbrella of a white birch. The high walls provide privacy as well as a clinging surface for lush greenery that adds to the romance.

GETAWAYS

Your backyard landscape is not only ideal for gathering; it also can provide the perfect spot for getting away. Finding a cozy corner to hang a hammock, place a bench, or set out a chaise longue creates a place to stop all activity and just kick back and relax. Even better, locate your getaway where you're shaded beneath a leafy bough or nestled up against a perimeter wall or high fence, or find a spot for an arbor or pergola sized just for an intimate two. Even in the tiniest yard, creating a spot that feels somewhat remote yet not too far from the action offers the delightful adult daydreaming place we all deserve.

above • A large property can enjoy multiple contemplative destinations, especially when there's a lovely pond to behold. This teak bench is strategically placed to take in the view.

left • A hemp hammock offers repose in a corner of the garden. Even if you rarely end up using it, it's great to know it's there.

Sometimes a little outbuilding can be turned into the perfect getaway. Here, a winding stepping stone path leads to a rustic bedroom nestled in the forest.

PLAY SPACES

We all know the many benefits of outdoor play, which include being active, collaborative, and imaginative. Now more than ever, our backyard landscapes need to draw kids outside so they can get away from computer and television screens and into nature once more.

Play spaces can be simple or elaborate, depending on budget, imagination, and inclination. You may choose to create a fairy-tale tree house, tempting hobbit hole, or simple sandbox . . . but if you don't, children will create their own from a low-hanging tree branch, the crawlspace under some overgrown shrubs, or a small muddy spot behind the garage. Just as old-time gardeners used to leave an untended corner for the fairies, make sure to leave a place in your yard for imaginative play. And remember that play is not just for children.

top right • This small backyard has just enough soft lawn space for kids to practice their headstands and somersaults. Adults can easily watch from the deck.

bottom right • This driveway offers space level and large enough for an indoor/outdoor ping-pong table. When folded up, it wheels right into the garage for storage.

facing page • This open platform built around a tree allows many kinds of physical play to happen in one place. A climbing rope, a hammock, a hauling bucket, and even a hopscotch court add to the fun of having a tree house in your own backyard.

Driveways and Garages

Driveways and garages—among the most utilitarian of landscape features—are not necessarily the most attractive, but thoughtful design can make them downright beautiful as well as useful.

If you are starting from scratch and can choose where to situate a driveway or garage, weigh the options very carefully—you will live with these choices every day. Where possible, locating the garage close to the kitchen of your house makes it easy to move kids, groceries, and trash between buildings. If unattached, building a roofed connection between garage and house keeps the path between the two dry and safe, especially in winter. Consider the shape of your driveway—a curved drive in front of the house can make the most of an underused front lawn, or a straight shot down the side of the property can be tucked out of the way, with access to side and back doors.

If you don't have the luxury of selecting the location of your driveway and garage, make the best of the existing plan by using plants to soften their appearance and make them part of the landscape. Add paths where needed to enhance access. The appearance of a garage can be altered with paint, different roofing material, or "jewelry" such as light fixtures, to better match your house and landscape.

Driveways can be of varied materials. Look for water-permeable options that reduce storm-water runoff; these can be among the most affordable paving options and include grass, gravel, stone, recycled plastic grid systems, permeable asphalt, pervious concrete, or good old-fashioned paving strips (see "Making Tracks," p. 48).

above • Here, the clean flat roof and wide opening of the attached garage meld well with the attractive terrace-like paving of the driveway.

above • A garage can double as a guest house or apartment under the eaves. This one sits far enough from the main house to enjoy privacy and views.

Turning a Driveway into a Garden

A derelict site was rejuvenated by the addition of a garage that feels like it has been set into a garden. Oversize granite pavers function as tire tracks softened by low plantings. The garage accommodates a car as well as a studio, a place for boat storage, and space for garden parties. While the house façade is aubergine, the garage was painted a complementary color, a buttery yellow that cheerfully welcomes one home.

right • **The flat black expanse of the old driveway looked like a no-man's-land between the home and its neighbor.**

below • **The space is nearly unrecognizable after the addition of the garage, driveway paving strips, and abundant plantings.**

BEFORE

A Charming Garage

On this central Ottawa (Canada) property, the detached garage and unavoidably long driveway presented a design challenge. Designer John Szczepaniak solved the problem by integrating the garage into the garden with an attached arbor and seating area; thus, the garage takes on the appearance of a charming garden building rather than a purely utilitarian structure.

The interlocking pavers of the driveway were set in a pattern that highlights the entrances and walkway along the side of the house. A small footbridge was built to link the driveway with an existing deck and create a distinct entrance into the oasis-like back garden. The paving pattern of the driveway and the railing of the footbridge mimic the design of a large window at the back of the house, marrying details of landscape and architecture.

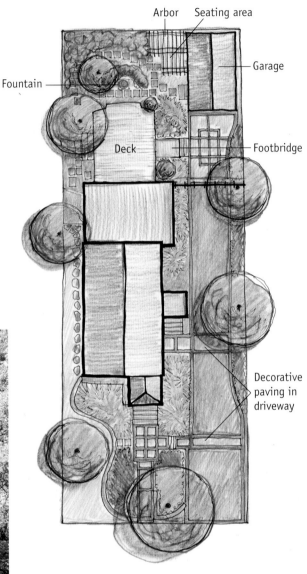

left · The driveway elegantly mirrors architectural features of the house, with pavers laid in a pattern that marks entry zones. The artful plantings of grasses such as feather reed grass (*Calamagrostis x acutiflora* 'Karl Foerster') help to bring the driveway into the landscape.

right · An ornamental grass (*Miscanthus sinensis* 'Autumn Light') is repeated on each side of the garage, while low ground covers tickle the pavers. The arbor over the driveway allows a curtain to be drawn across it during parties, providing additional entertaining space in front of the garage.

below · The arbor attached to the side of the garage creates an intimate seating area perfect for viewing the garden and a water feature.

Making Tracks

Like many once-common things whose modern-day replacements proved expensive or environmentally unsound, driveway paving strips are back in vogue. Paving strips are bands of paving materials just wide enough for a car's tires and can be made of recycled, poured, or dimensional concrete, thick stone pavers, cobblestones, brick, or gravel. The strips' surrounds can be planted in low, tough ground covers that can stand heavy foot traffic as people get in and out of vehicles. Best of all, these plantings act as pervious sponges so that water runoff doesn't overwhelm storm drains in the street.

1. Pavers are interplanted with flowering moss (*Sagina subulata*) and periwinkle (*Vinca minor*) with its resilient dark-green foliage and cornflower blue flowers. 2. Concrete paving stones and tidy grass planting strips complement this house's neat lines. 3. Long slabs of poured concrete present a clean appearance when highlighted by mounding ground covers that surround stepping stones of recycled concrete. 4. Beachside communities use local crushed oyster shells as a sustainable path and driveway solution.

OPEN-AIR

You can make a living, dining, lounging—even sleeping—space outside,

just as you do inside.

ROOMS

Getting Some Air

While an outdoor room can be just about anywhere on your property, the most traditional is an attached porch. As a part of the house itself, a porch usually sits under an extension of the roof and is well protected from the elements. It abuts at least one wall of the house and is often built at the same floor level as inside, so it's easy to transition in and out. A porch can sit on the front, side, or back of the house, be narrow or wide, and be open or screened to keep out insects. This is the place where you can really live in the out-of-doors, where comfortable wicker or teak furniture with over-stuffed pillows draws you out to a cool shady spot.

Unless protected by an awning or shade structure, a deck or patio sits out under the sky. Constructed of wood, steel, or recycled materials, a deck is an extension of the house that can be built on top of a roof, to the side of a building, or even on the ground as a low platform. A patio is usually a level piece of ground on which a paved surface sits. It can extend the inside of a house out into the landscape as a large area for seating or act like a floating island in the midst of plantings or lawn. Paving options are plentiful.

Open-air rooms can also be constructed around swimming pools, hot tubs, and even outdoor showers—anywhere water can be enjoyed. A hard surface underfoot usually helps to keep wet feet from tracking dirt or grass clippings everywhere. But sometimes you might prefer an outdoor room with a verdant soft carpet underfoot—a well-clipped lawn or mossy glade offers a spot for picnicking or leisurely lounging on the grass.

These days, sheds are used for tool and garden equipment storage, animal shelter, or even as a get-away space for work or for play. These mini-houses, when well designed, draw the eye and the foot, attracting children and the child in all of us to snuggle in for awhile.

left · A roofed deck adds expansive living—and dining—space outside the walls of this house. Hinged panels of glass open wide to let in light and air, making for an easy passage between inside and out.

below · Floor-to-ceiling screened frames open up views from porch to garden, just like a Japanese screen.

Swaths of plantings form the walls, a leafy bough creates the ceiling, and a circle of flat fieldstone becomes the floor of this charming open-air room. At its center sits a white wrought-iron table and chairs, poised and ready.

Porches

A porch feels simultaneously like a part of the house and a part of the landscape: a place perched somewhere in between. You can entertain, dine, and even sleep out on a porch, feeling close to the elements while in a protected place.

Because most porches are not closed-in structures that are built to keep out all kinds of weather, materials need to be weather-resistant, thoughtfully detailed, and built to last. Since rain and snow can accumulate on its roof, a porch needs to adhere to appropriate moisture-proofing, flashing, and guttering standards to keep water where it belongs: outside the structure. Rain chains and gutters can deposit water into rain gardens, but choosing local hardwoods like cedar or exotic woods like ipé and finishing them with a moisture-proof stain will help maintain the structure, no matter the weather event. Caulking joints to keep water from getting inside any structure is imperative in an indoor/outdoor environment.

Similarly, you need to think about moisture issues as you choose your porch flooring. Mortared stone or brick works well outside, as does stained concrete. Wood finished with either a clear stain or a deck paint can hold up under rigorous weather conditions; with proper maintenance you'll enjoy your porch for years to come.

right • This colorfully painted porch is a true open-air room: It's built into the structure of the house with only some posts and a railing separating it from the garden level below.

facing page, top • Where to put the grill? Two steps bring you down to the outdoor kitchen where the griller can talk with guests while attending to the tasks at hand.

facing page, bottom • The girth of these columns and the maturity of the plantings create the feeling that you're inside a giant terrarium.

SCREENED PORCHES

On a hot summer's day, who wouldn't love curling up with a good book and a cold beverage on an old settee in a screened porch with an overhead fan moving the air around, just right, protected from the elements and marauding insects as you look out onto your landscape through a shimmering screen. It's hard to imagine a more relaxing scenario.

A well-designed screened porch can serve as protected outdoor dining, living, and play space, or even as a sleeping room. With a solid roof overhead, either floor-to-ceiling screens or screens over well-caulked half-walls, and stone or wood flooring underfoot (important tip: make sure to screen the space between the floorboards to keep the mosquitoes out), a screened porch lets you live in the out-of-doors from late spring through early fall.

top right • People with screened porches often move in for the summer. Being so close to nature while the weather's good is like camping, except with a full kitchen and other amenities close at hand.

bottom right • Supporting posts help to frame distant views, breaking the landscape into parts the way a delicate folding screen does. The stone floor is an extension of the patio outside the screens.

facing page • So many places to sit, so little time! Depending on the season, you can dine outside beneath the pergola or lounge inside the screened porch.

Decks

Much like a porch, a deck is a floored structure that adjoins a house, but without the overhead protection of a roof. Because they perch on top of or at the edge of a landscape, decks can seem to float on high, perfect for basking in the sun or relaxing under the stars. Some decks sit on supporting posts; others cantilever beyond.

When designed thoughtfully, railings not only protect people from falling over the edge but also enable viewers to see through to the landscape below. Make sure to adhere to local building codes as you design your railing. Standard heights, spacing, and diameters of openings create a belt of safety around your deck.

above • Stainless steel cables strung between supporting posts enable loungers to view the landscape beyond.

left • Roof decks bring us right up under the sky. Here, a fireplace provides warmth and a dancing focal point.

facing page, bottom • Thick stacked-stone piers provide a stable base for this cantilevered deck, in stark contrast with the thin stainless steel railings and staircase.

Sustainable Decking Options

These days there are many ways to go green when it comes to choosing decking materials. One way is to source sustainably harvested wood that has been certified by the Forest Stewardship Council (FSC), whose guidelines set out responsible forestry practices. Locally harvested redwood or cedar also make an excellent choice.

Another way is to choose composite decking made from a combination of recycled plastic and waste wood fibers, an excellent long-lasting alternative. Other materials include PVC or aluminum decking, both of which are fully recyclable. If you're really resourceful, consider recycling salvage lumber as decking.

An Updated Arbor

On this deep, narrow lot in New Haven, Conn., multiple utilitarian functions are achieved in a carefully planned design. The pergola-shaded deck, located just off the kitchen, offers space for outdoor dining and entertaining. Privacy—and air flow—are maintained by the inclusion of a high slatted fence that abuts deck and house, and a stainless steel cable fence enables diners to look into the sunny patio and garden four steps below.

The backyard contains a shade garden under a mature tree and raised vegetable beds tucked behind the garage. This small back yard, designed by AKV Architects, uses every square inch to turn a once-derelict space into an urban oasis.

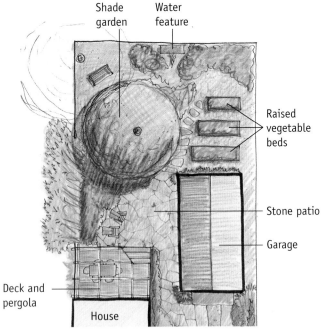

left · Aluminum dining chairs and table nestle into the corner of the wooden deck. Slender white columns not only provide structural support for the pergola overhead, but also act as fence posts for the high slatted privacy fence on the property line.

facing page • Thin cable railings strung within a steel frame nearly disappear from view, maintaining a clear visual connection between deck, patio, and garden in this small urban backyard.

right • While the house hasn't changed much, the backyard has. An unpainted wooden pergola supported grapevines, but no back door provided access to get there.

below • A high horizontally slatted wooden fence brings both security and privacy to this urban backyard. To the left of the deck, a door replaces a window, making the flow between inside and out smooth and efficient.

BEFORE

Patios

A patio is an outdoor living space that sits directly on the ground. Often built adjacent to a house or other structure, a patio is usually made of some kind of paving material that makes a clean, level surface underfoot, allowing for easy movement of furniture and people.

Patios are defined as paved areas that adjoin a building, but they also include mosaic-filled courtyards at the center of a complex of buildings. Favored by southern climates as a means to regulate sun and shade throughout the day, these courtyards bring light and air and offer a realm of quiet solitude for their users.

above • Gravel works well as a patio surface, particularly when used on a rooftop as an inexpensive solution to drainage and weight issues.

Random rectangular patterned bluestone makes a handsome terrace, especially when set off by edging of the same material.

Large slabs of quarried granite create a stark star-shaped terrace set into a copse of tall, thin deciduous trees.

Outdoor Living at Its Best

When an Ottawa (Canada) couple completed an extensive renovation of their home, the house was noticeably at odds with its drab, undesigned setting. Landscape architect John Szczepaniak developed an intimate set of patios that provides a restful haven in the midst of a central neighborhood.

At the heart of this open-air room is a beloved crab apple tree, visible from the kitchen windows, which provides food for the birds and a fragrant canopy over the lower terrace. The space was graded to accommodate the tree, and square-cut limestone paving stones, pea gravel, and planting beds replaced the uninviting lawn.

The garden's sleek, geometric design takes its contemporary flair from the modern kitchen. The playful patterning of the fence, repeated in the custom grill table outside the kitchen door, provides visual interest.

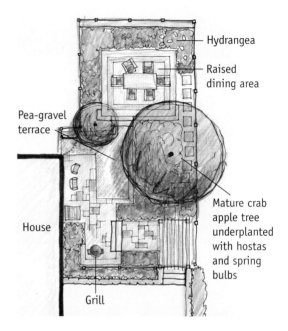

Hydrangea

Raised dining area

Pea-gravel terrace

Mature crab apple tree underplanted with hostas and spring bulbs

House

Grill

above • The pea-gravel terrace is not only a low-maintenance lawn alternative, but also provides an inviting space for seating and grilling. The doorway from the driveway into the garden was intentionally aligned with the crab apple tree, to showcase the tree's year-round beauty.

right • The little terrace outside the kitchen could barely accommodate two chairs, while the much-used grill sat alone in a patch of lawn.

facing page • The raised dining area at the back features a beautiful mature hydrangea saved from the original yard. The fence design echoes light fixtures on the outside of the house and is made of an easy-care weathered cedar punctuated with panels of opaque Acrylite®.

BEFORE

Paving Options

How you choose to pave your terrace is bound only by your imagination. Traditional materials like brick, bluestone, sandstone, and flat fieldstone are now augmented by contemporary concrete applications, such as concrete pavers, tinted poured concrete, and stamped concrete in a host of patterns.

CLAY BRICK
$-$$

- Easy to install on a well-prepared base, maintenance free, lasts for generations
- Aged brick available at many salvage yards
- Use in a variety of patterns like these brick squares bounded by wide cracks filled with moss

CONCRETE PAVERS
$-$$

- Clean, smooth look; easy-to-sweep patio
- Economical; easy installation
- Base should be prepared well to avoid cracking
- Concrete can break down over time

RECTANGULAR PAVERS
$$-$$$

- Joints can be tight or open with grass or ground cover
- Larger stones are heavy and may require a professional to install
- Available in natural stone or prefabricated options

MORTARED RIVERSTONE AND PAVERS
$$-$$$

- Mixing materials allows for creativity and resourcefulness
- Using different materials may be more difficult to install
- Mortared riverstones as seen here are not suitable for zones where the ground freezes

NATURAL STONE FLAGGING
$$-$$$

- Rustic/informal look with a variety of sizes and stone types
- Larger joints can be planted with grass or ground covers

CLAY BRICK

CAST-IN-PLACE AND TINTED CONCRETE PAVERS

RECTANGULAR PAVERS

MORTARED RIVERSTONE AND PAVERS

NATURAL STONE FLAGGING

Lawns

When designed thoughtfully, your lawn can function as an open-air room that works as well for lounging and entertaining as it does for play. Grassy areas are a place where kids can kick a ball around, play tag, make a fort, or do somersaults. As with a glade in a forest, a lawn also serves to bring light and air into the property. Design your lawn as a "pool of space"--a continuous surface that is framed, like a swimming pool, by a clear edge. This will turn what seemed like leftover space into a handsome focal area of your landscape.

above • When crisply defined by a path, curb, or metal edging, a panel of lawn creates a geometric open space that provides a handsome frame for the house and a place to play in the front yard.

above • Grass underfoot can serve as a verdant terrace for garden furniture and al fresco dining.

left • A grass bocce court edged in boxwood serves both as playspace and verdant corridor terminated by a handsome Chippendale bench.

This grassy oval acts as a visual relief space in the midst of abundant plantings.

Pools

A swimming pool can be designed as a handsome horizontal focal point around which the surrounding spaces are organized. Most pools are formed from concrete shells topped by stone coping that acts as a frame for the water. If the pool is painted a dark color, like gray or black, the water reflects the sky; if painted turquoise to match the sky, then the two can seem to meld together as one. Both are attractive effects.

These days, pools are usually formed using a concrete Gunite® method that allows different shapes and edgings to be created. Another important development in pool design is the automatic pool cover that works on a rectangular-shaped pool to keep children safe, intruders out, and evaporation to a minimum.

GREEN IDEAS THAT WORK

Chlorine Alternatives

Because chlorine by-products have been linked to higher incidences of asthma, miscarriages, and cancer, new greener methods of disinfecting pools are also changing the way people swim. Ozonators combined with in-floor cleaners keep water clean with a minimum of chemical treatment. Saltwater pools are also popular, designed to reduce micro-organisms to a safe level. Ultraviolet disinfection systems add a layer of protection by oxidizing organic contaminants.

Shallow wading pools and swim spas bring the right amount of water into small backyards.

Swim spas are small pools built for exercising against an artificially generated current. This pool is set into a freestanding limestone wall that supports a small raised terrace area.

right • With the press of a button, an automatic pool cover glides into action. Not only is increased safety a big benefit, but limiting evaporation also means water is conserved. Using less energy to run the circulation system and reducing overall maintenance are also pluses.

below • This swimming pool is designed to look like a natural pond. A hillside of shrubs and trees, with abundant plantings in poolside pockets, transforms this space into a verdant oasis.

HOT TUBS & SPAS

For those living in northern climates, a hot tub is one of the best ways to relax in the out-of-doors, especially in the dead of winter. Others tout the therapeutic benefits from the spray jets that can be set to massage different parts of the body. With temperatures as high as 105°F, these small pools can be built of wood with staves (like a barrel), concrete Gunite, or one-piece stainless steel or acrylic and are powered by wood, gas, or electricity. Solar hot water systems are also possible in certain climates.

Whatever style hot tub you select, make sure to locate it close to an area in your house with a bath or changing room. While some people prefer to place it under cover of a roof or pergola, others like to use it as a nighttime retreat under the stars. When easily reached, a hot tub acts as a warm and comfortable "away room," even in the most inclement weather.

The path to a spa should be easily maintained and shoveled. Putting hooks nearby for robes or towels is a small but important detail. It's also a wonderful viewing position to look out on the rest of your landscape, so installing night lighting can enhance your hot tub experience.

top right · This in-ground spa, complete with automatic cover, incorporates hydrojets that ease back and neck pain. This mini-pool is also the focal point of a hedged garden room.

bottom right · Portable home spas are easily available and quickly installed onsite. Measuring about 7½ ft. square, they can be eyesores in a landscape if not thoughtfully designed. This hot tub sits adjacent to the house on a throne-like deck and terrace.

OUTDOOR SHOWERS

There is a freedom that comes from showering in the out-of-doors. For those lucky enough to have a pool or pond on their property or a beach nearby, it's helpful to have access to an outdoor area to clean or towel off before setting foot inside. A simple showerhead, some paving underfoot, a way to drain the water, and a screen or fence for privacy that allows air to circulate easily are just about all you need.

top left • Placing an outdoor shower right under a porch ceiling and on an exterior wall is a great way to use leftover space while ensuring privacy, whatever the time of day.

bottom left • Air circulation is always important to consider when installing an outdoor shower. Slats break up one's view while allowing cooling breezes within.

below • This charming spiral shower shields the body while allowing views out. And it looks like fun.

Sheds and Outbuildings

Sheds are little houses that serve a needed function in our backyard landscapes. Tool sheds, chicken houses, gazebos, meditation huts, even an outdoor workroom are all typical uses of a shed. Often designed to be a mini-version of the larger residence, a shed can be located near the main house or at a remote corner of the property. When that happens, it functions as an eye-catcher as well as a destination that draws people into the landscape.

top right · Linked to the main house by a shade structure, this tiny shed might function as a tool shed, a writer's cottage, or a changing room. The rocking chair, hammock, and dining set all suggest that it's a home away from home.

bottom right · A hidden door in a fence is the only giveaway that there's a utility shed behind it. We all possess things to store outside but rarely do it so elegantly.

below · Setting your shed at the far edge of your property makes it feel as though it's remote, while drawing the eye—and foot—to visit.

above top · Climbing hydrangea vine has overtaken this tool shed, showing the horticultural bias of its owner.

above bottom · This little shed was designed to be a mini version of its parent—the main house. Sheds and little houses look best when something, whether trim or body color, roof pitch, or detailing, relates back to a larger structure nearby.

top right · A classical Greek garden house is an eyecatcher with columns, pediment, and windows; an elegant focal point in the middle of this vegetable garden of raised beds.

bottom right · Some people live or work in their sheds. This Japanesque structure, set in a forest, could function as a summer pavilion, meditation hut, or picnic destination.

Open-Air Rooms 75

Shade Structures

As our globe continues to heat up and more and more people face drought conditions, regulating the light overhead in our open-air rooms is vital to our comfort while outdoors and to our overall enjoyment of nature. For one thing, creating a "ceiling" for our outdoor rooms limits and defines the vast space above and creates a sense of intimacy below. Retractable awnings allow homeowners to protect what's beneath from the sun and when necessary from the rain; openwork pergolas baffle and break up the sun's rays, while letting weather and cooling breezes through.

Practical issues aside, there are plenty of aesthetic reasons to use overhead enclosures. Handsome patterns of dappled light are cast upon the furniture and floor below; when combined with leafy climbing vines, an overhead garden or orchard is created. Place your dining table underneath a grape arbor, and pluck away.

above · Although this pergola sits high above the tile-topped table, the close spacing of the boards overhead helps cast a deep shade over the whole.

left · A shade structure can be made into a weather-resistant outdoor room by placing translucent fiberglass panels overhead.

facing page · Without this pergola made of cedar poles that rest atop stone piers, this high-walled outdoor room would be too hot for sitting.

East Meets West

This northern California landscape represents innovative design on a realistic budget. The owner wanted clean, simple lines in keeping with the modern Asian-inspired design of his remodeled ranch home. Landscape designer Patricia St. John created a sustainable, elegant retreat perfect for the client's aesthetic sensibilities and love of entertaining.

Creatively recycling materials from the existing deck, she flipped over boards to build a smaller deck, stained a warm, rich hue. The concrete patio was sawn into strips and laid out in a geometric design of raked sand, black La Paz rock, and decorative stone mulch. Nylon "sails" overhead provide shade with dramatic flair, at a minimal cost. At the back of the property, framed openings were cut in the back fence to provide a view of the creek beyond and to visually expand the space. Grasses were a natural choice as plant material: elegant, low-maintenance, and drought-tolerant.

top right • Strung from the posts of an old arbor, the "sails" can be retracted when more sun is wanted or when the portable firepit is in use. The steps are recycled rafters from the arbor.

bottom right • The open design is highly conducive to entertaining; the interior designer put wheels on the dining room table so that it could be moved outside for al fresco dining. The fence openings have 3-in. x 3-in. wire inset for security while allowing views of the creek and vegetation beyond the yard.

A thirsty, high-maintenance lawn was eliminated, replaced by a geometric design of concrete, sand, and stone, punctuated by ceramic balls and plantings of cape rushes (*Chondropetalum tectorum*), Berkeley sedge (*Carex divulsa*), and other grasses.

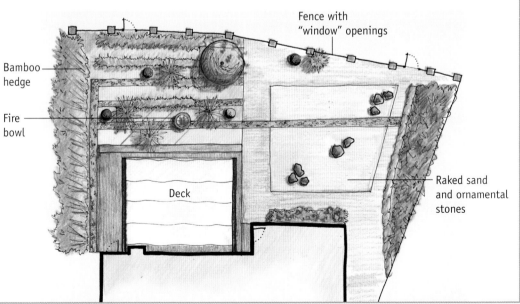

Bamboo hedge

Fire bowl

Fence with "window" openings

Deck

Raked sand and ornamental stones

WALLS,

When outdoor spaces are outlined by a wall, fence,

FENCES,

or hedge, they become places we seek to inhabit.

AND HEDGES

Enclosures

An enclosure, like a wall, fence, screen, or hedge, designates and defines an outside area as special. Such boundaries have always played an important functional role in the landscape: to keep livestock in and intruders out. These days, an enclosure can also be used to mark property lines, close in a hazard like a swimming pool, and provide privacy.

An enclosure also acts to extend the walls of the house out into the landscape. It's strange but true: an enclosed space feels larger than a similar area lacking such definition. Perhaps it's because a fenced yard seems like it's marked out as special, with its clear edges and entrance gate.

There are many ways to create enclosures in your landscape. Walls, built of stone, concrete, or other masonry materials, bring a solid structural presence to a front or back yard. Wooden, steel, or bamboo fences sit more lightly on the land and are less expensive to erect but don't last as long as their masonry counterparts. Hedges are the least expensive means of enclosing a landscape. Evergreen or deciduous, tall or low, hedges can be effective living screens for a variety of settings. Gateways, as breaks in an enclosure, allow passage into the delineated realm. Railings are low post and rail structures designed to keep people from falling over an edge, especially on stairways or around high decks.

The simplest kind of enclosure—edging—separates plants or garden beds from pathways or lawns in a useful and attractive way.

above • An ornate wrought-iron gateway, in line with an elegant double staircase leading into the house, links lawn areas separated by stone walls and hedges.

right • Dry-laid stone walls are an ancient form of enclosure, built originally to use up excess material, delineate boundaries, and keep in livestock. These days, we enjoy them for their beauty and sense of history.

above • A wrought-iron handrail softened by a leafy vine embraces this outdoor living room.

left • This 7-ft.-high fence is made of a series of concrete-block piers and wire mesh panels that keep animals out, allow air circulation through, and provide views into the forest beyond.

Walls

Walls are powerful visual extensions of the architecture of your house into the landscape. They can be structural or ornamental and can serve different purposes in the landscape. Structural walls are often used to retain soil. Where the ground slopes but a level area is needed, retaining walls are added to terrace the area. Freestanding walls sit above the ground and can be seen from both sides. These can provide backdrops to gardens, define the edge of the property, create a sense of privacy, or frame an opening for a driveway or path.

An interesting form can give walls greater character. Straight walls are practical, direct, and efficient. Curved walls, with their softer flow, can be playful, meandering, or sensuous. Tall walls that you can't see over or where a lot of soil is being retained can be intimidating. A friendly height for a wall is one that allows a neighborly view between houses.

Materials and finish details can make all the difference. Whether stucco or stone, mortared or dry stacked, round or square stone, natural or cut stone cap, stucco texture and color, there are countless details that you can use to give a wall your own personal touch.

top right · Concrete walls that are plastered or stuccoed can resemble traditional hand-molded adobe or mud walls. Vivid colors satisfy in this tropical setting.

bottom right · Irregular blocks of limestone are stacked to form a low planter wall. Use local stone wherever possible.

above · These walls retain a steep slope, creating terraced spaces for trees and large shrubs. Make sure to include weep holes behind the walls to allow water to drain through.

left · This wall is built of concrete faced with stone and capped with a contrasting material, in this case, bluestone. A slightly higher square pier provides a clear end to the wall, marks the top landing for the steps, and provides a base for the Arts and Crafts lantern that lights the way.

STONE WALLS

Many of us are lucky to live where natural stone is plentiful. Whether flat or rounded, granite, sandstone, or limestone, a stone wall made out of what's local looks great because it is in keeping with the natural landscape. And there are many ways to build with stone. You can use round or flat fieldstones to face a wall or to create a built-up surface. Joints between stones can be fully mortared, partially mortared (hidden joints), or dry-laid (where no mortar is used at all). Make sure you employ an experienced mason to get the best results.

facing page, top • This arching picket fence sits directly on a concrete wall faced with a thin veneer of fieldstone.

facing page, bottom • This dry stone wall was built without mortar. At its end, a ruin-like window seems to erupt from a sea of plantings.

above • A steeply sloping hillside can be held back by building stone retaining walls. Properly engineered, they act as beautifully planted terraces that create more usable living space.

right • Wide stone walls curve between upper and lower lawn areas. Flat fieldstones are secured in place using a dark-tinted mortar instead of a cap.

A Green Wall

A recent Boston-area JMMDS project aimed to turn a high retaining wall along a tight entry space into a lovely vertical garden. To do this, we proposed transforming one side of this shady driveway into a living wall. A steel frame made of cells to hold soil was bolted into a 7-ft.-high, curving concrete retaining wall and then filled with a palette of predominantly native, shade-loving perennials. Now this north-facing space functions as an outdoor entryway, a driveway turnaround or parking spot, a protected place to read a book, and also a living work of garden art that greets the homeowners whenever they come home.

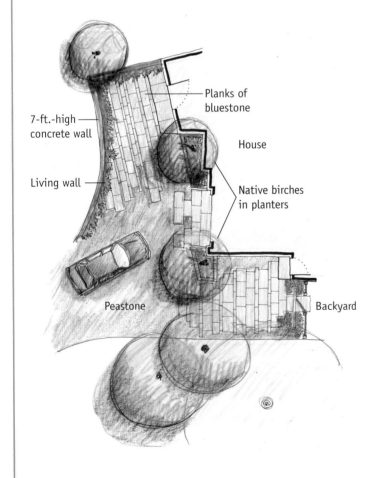

7-ft.-high concrete wall

Living wall

Planks of bluestone

House

Native birches in planters

Peastone

Backyard

above • Ferns (both Christmas and autumn), Solomon seal (*Polygonatum commutatum*), woodland strawberry (*Fragaria vesca*), bunchberry dogwood (*Cornus canadensis*), fringed bleeding heart (*Dicentra eximia*), and wintergreen (*Gaultheria procumbens*) grace this north-facing green wall.

left • Native birch trees (*Betula papyrifera*) in the entry planters add a forest feel while veiling the height of the four-story Silver LEED-certified residence. Handsome planks of Alcove bluestone are set into a sea of peastone that together make a permeable surface able to bear the weight of cars.

TILED WALLS

For those who live in southern climes, the bright sun and warm weather offer opportunities to bring color into your open-air rooms. Artfully designed tiled walls can act as vertical focal points with their planes of smooth, colorful finishes that catch the light and make for an easy-to-clean, moisture-proof surface.

Tile can be laid out as a background that highlights a fountain or sculpture or as a focal point in itself. Colorful tiles made of glass, ceramic, or natural stone are all available in a wide range of sizes and finishes. You can even design your own tile pattern, putting your personal stamp on your backyard.

above • Large squares of blue tile are used to face an exterior planter wall filled with native plantings, enclosing an ipé deck.

left • Vivid colors stand out in bright light. Flanked by fig trees and agaves, the tile pattern on this wall acts like a hearth in a living room, creating a central focal point around which to place the furniture.

A palette of fieldstone, stucco, and tile blend together around a fountain, helping make this arched courtyard feel cool in a hot climate.

SEATING WALLS

A seating wall is a masonry wall built at a height and depth to provide a place to sit. Retaining and freestanding walls alike can deliver a solid bench for sitting. Since stone can be hard to sit on and cold to the touch, seat walls can be made more comfortable by the addition of a wooden seat or cushions, or when painted in light colors or softened by cascading plants. Typical seat heights can be as low as 12 in. and as high as 30 in. (more of a leaning height), with the usual height being 18 in. or so from the ground.

above • A low concrete wall whose limestone cap doubles as a circular seat retains this island planting and breaks up the expanse of a large concrete driveway.

left • A skilled mason fashioned a built-in seat out of a retaining wall, complete with a side table for setting drinks or containers of plants.

facing page • An exedra—a semicircular bench—fits perfectly around a firepit that also functions as a coffee table. The thick pillows made of outdoor fabric bring the feeling of inside out. Notice the handsome bevel formed along the inside edge of the bench.

Terracing down the Slope

This riverfront property in New York's Thousand Islands had a complicated grade, and bedrock underneath the entire property limited the capacity to grow deep-rooted plants. Landscape architect Mariane Wheatley-Miller created a series of seven linked terraces leading from the house down to the water and boathouse. The hand-built walls and stair facings were made of local stone, and bluestone pavers were used for the patios and steps. Plant material was chosen carefully for its hardiness, as well as its billowing and softening effect on the stone hardscape.

right • Climbing and clinging vines soften the stone walls throughout the property.

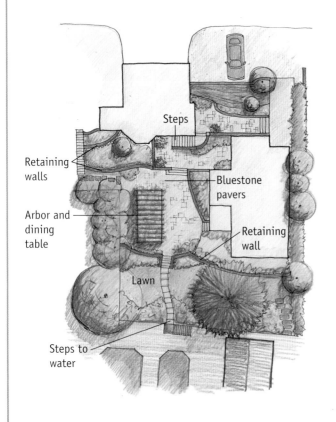

above • The dining area under a large-scale arbor is shaded by wisteria vine. A stately line of river birches (*Betula nigra* 'Heritage') mirrors the arbor's supports.

above • A softly curving retaining wall forms one of the terraces that turns this steep slope into usable living space.

Wall Materials

Walls define a space. Whether they are freestanding, to screen or divide a space, or retaining, to create levels in your garden, walls make landscapes more interesting and dynamic. You can sit on them, install plants that will climb up them, or create curves or angles with them. There are a multitude of contemporary and traditional products to choose from. Use a licensed contractor to install walls that are higher than 24 in.

PRECAST BLOCK

PRECAST BLOCK
$

- Available in an array of earth tones, with textured, flat, or curved face
- Easy, modular installation
- Maintenance free
- Capstone necessary

STUCCO
$$

- Clean, contemporary look; virtually any color possible
- Concrete block or poured internal wall requires professional installation
- Stucco will need to be reapplied over time

BRICK
$$

- Timeless appeal; colors are limited to clay and gray tones but don't fade
- Create a variety of patterns like running bond, basketweave, or jack-on-jack
- Taller walls should be installed by a professional

VENEER
$$

- Thin stone installed onto concrete base gives the look of natural stone, but is easier to install and less expensive
- Capstone necessary

FIELDSTONE
$$-$$$

- Variations in size, coloring, and stacking styles
- May require professional installation
- Can be installed with or without cap, with or without mortar

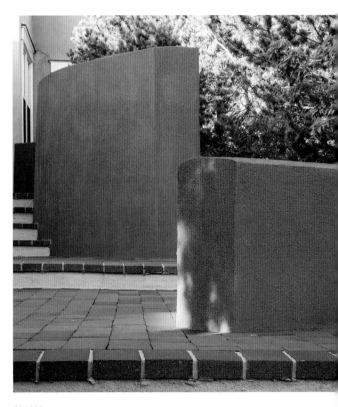

STUCCO

BRICK

VENEER

FIELDSTONE

Fences

Fences have distinct personalities of their own, whether they are mainly functional or more decorative. When a property needs a fence, it can be an opportunity to make it a feature—something special in the landscape.

An open patterned fence is often used when separation is needed but privacy is not. Picket and split rail fences are light and delicate. Solid fences provide privacy and security. These no-nonsense enclosures don't need to be plain; there are many materials, colors, patterns, and finish details for added interest.

Fences often emphasize straight lines—vertically and horizontally—in the landscape. Yet a fence needs to address the slope of the ground. Sections of fencing can either step up or down or slope to follow the grade. Following a curve, like along a road, the sections can zigzag perpendicular to each other, for a crisp look. Fences with curved sections must be custom designed, and they add a tailored look to any landscape.

Materials, colors, and patterns bring variety. For wooden fences, the scale and size of the posts and boards makes a difference; the sturdier the posts and boards, the stronger the fence. Weather-resistant woods are the best choice if a natural finish is desired. Painting or staining can offer different finished looks, each with their own maintenance needs.

Patterns in fences vary, from the spindles of a wrought-iron fence to the tops of pickets to the toppers of stockade fences. Lattice, cutouts, or custom patterning in the topmost section of a fence can bring a decorative element to a landscape. A good rule is to have the top pattern be no more than one-third of the overall height of the fence.

above • Add some bright colors to a simple pine board fence and you create an exuberant backyard that draws you outside while providing privacy from neighbors' eyes.

right • This board fence moves down the slope in repeating steps, while the location of the decorative Chinese-style panel stays the same.

above • The house is nearly obscured by a lilac (*Syringa vulgaris*) planting behind a spindle fence that is set on top of a masonry wall.

right • Wooden fencing steps up a sloping sidewalk in regular increments. Each panel is protected by a small roof over an openwork topper. Spacers between the boards allow air to circulate into the garden. A handsome gate, halfway up the hill announces the entry.

FENCE CLIMBERS

You can add a living layer to your fence by planting a vine nearby that can twine its way across it. Grape and hops vines are vigorous growers, as are flowering favorites like clematis, trumpet vines, and wisteria. When you plant climbers on a solid board fence, you'll need to provide small nails or screws for twining; on an openwork screen, the vines will usually weave through openings on their own. Another way to veil a tall fence is to plant an espalier—often a fruit tree that's been trained to a flat plane—in front of it.

right • This fence, made of woven steel, emphasizes the horizontal and provides structure for climbing vines.

below • Grapevine, a vigorous grower, tendrils up this slatted fence. The crisp white posts bring a clean contrast to the 3-in. boards set ½ in. apart for movement of light and air.

This espaliered tree is composed of different apple stock grafted onto a main stem. Over time, each branch can be trained to grow along the wooden fence, bringing beauty and edible delight to its owner.

Hedges

A hedge planting is one way to build an enclosure without breaking the bank. It can be made of evergreen materials, like an arborvitae hedge; deciduous plants, like a lilac or privet hedge; or even a mixed planting that combines both.

Some hedging materials, like privet or boxwood, look best when sheared or hand-pruned regularly to maintain an appropriate size and breadth. Other live screening looks good when left to grow to its natural height, such as lilac and rhododendron hedges.

Mixed hedges add variety in color and texture; imagine evergreens growing with climbing roses and a contrasting foliage shrub. Given the right growing conditions, and depending on the plant selection, most hedges will mature quickly.

above · Because it is so easy to prune, boxwood is a satisfying hedging material that can be trimmed into architectural or curving shapes. In this garden, it acts as a soft low wall that encloses more shrubs that billow above it.

left · Flowering hydrangea hedges encircle a small bluestone patio, creating a low enclosure, while a high privet hedge screens out neighbors.

facing page · This elegant bamboo hedge (*Bambusa multiplex* 'Alphonse Karr') grows to a neat 7-ft. height. Clumping bamboos, unlike running bamboos, will stay within their bounds.

Gateways

A gateway marks an opening in an enclosure and a threshold into the landscape. Designed thoughtfully, it can beckon to a stroller to enter the realm within.

Sometimes gates are designed to look continuous with their neighboring fence, built of the same materials and patterns in order to blend in with the surroundings. Piers, special columns, or a change in height, style, or color are all ways to turn a break in a wall or fence into the highlight of an enclosure. Building a pergola or trellis overhead can also help distinguish an opening from its surroundings. When planted with a flowering vine that tendrils above, a gateway provides visitors with a delightful garden experience.

A subtle but important detail is to place a large threshold stone under the gateway opening to indicate that this is a place to pause and appreciate the landscape ahead. When possible, locate any steps away from the gateway opening since stepping up or down while operating a gate can be tricky.

top right • Handsome finial-topped wooden posts interrupt this continuous line of pointed pickets. Diagonal bracing keeps a gate's frame square to the post so it's easy to open.

bottom right • An inexpensive split-rail fence backed with welded wire fabric provides a clean enclosure for this horse paddock.

left • The handsome wooden gate marks the entry to a stone staircase. The retaining walls are made of rough stone that contrasts well with the smooth painted finish of the gate.

below • The patterning of this fence and gate provide the structure for growing hops vines (*Humulus lupulus*). The path material flows out below the gate, indicating where to enter.

A Birdhouse Post

Fences need many posts in order to support them and keep them standing (especially when on a curve, as in the example shown). Why not have them do double duty and use one, or even many, of them as a birdhouse as well?

Railings

Railings are vital to our sense of security in a landscape, helping to keep us from falling while standing or traveling on steps, decks, and balconies. They are particularly important as handholds in periods of inclement weather and as we age. They can help lead a visitor physically and visually into a landscape, or can seem to disappear to allow us to appreciate the view beyond.

Railings can complement adjacent gardens. When painted a similar color to the house body or trim, they extend its presence into the landscape. When stained a natural color, they tend to blend in more with their surroundings.

Railings often are designed with a pattern or repeating rhythm that can be a strong element in the landscape. When surrounding a deck, many railings interrupt our view of the world beyond. However, new stainless steel or cable systems provide enclosure while seeming to disappear from view. Always check local building codes to learn the particular conditions—height, opening size, and materials— for which a railing can be installed.

above • This wooden railing meets the building code while allowing a view of the landscape beyond.

DETAILS THAT WORK

Painted Handrail

This handsome painted handrail is angled so that one can easily slide a hand along it down the long flight of stairs. With stairs, steps, or other level changes, the design of the handrails should follow the slope at a consistent height from the ground or staircase. The vertical rhythm of the railing contrasts with the horizontal lines of the stone wall and stairs beyond. This creates a sense of cohesion between the different materials, without too much repetition.

above • These stainless steel railings seem to disappear into the landscape. Contemporary cable systems have changed the way we enjoy our decks.

left • A painted wooden handrail helps people navigate this angular walk down the stairs. A closet pole or dowel attached on the inside offers a handhold along the way and gives the clematis vine a little more room to grow.

Edging

When you edge your walkway, garden bed, or lawn area, you create a clean, crisp demarcation that satisfies our need for definition in a landscape. Like a molding strip or a border on a wooden floor, creating a frame around a space, however subtle, brings it into focus.

You can make an edging using a border of boxwood or other low hedge, cobblestone or brick, pressure-treated lumber set lengthwise, roofing tile, plastic edging, or even just by spading an edge to separate bed from lawn—creating a continuous and distinctive line around a pool of space.

above • A "river" of lawn edged by cobblestones is reinforced by a band of double white New Guinea Impatiens (*Impatiens hawkeri*).

left • A stone retaining wall acts as an edging between a hillside of roses and a sidewalk. An errant rose bough cascades down to the street level, bringing a delightful blurring to the border.

Extruded concrete curbing creates a clean, flowing edge for this stabilized soil walkway. Concrete is fed into an extruding machine, then compacted and fed out through the chosen mold with control joints cut every 3 ft.

Finished Edges

Just as piping or a band of grosgrain ribbon provides a clean finish to a seam on a dress, so an edge in a garden acts as a way to detail a design.

SPADED EDGE

- A spaded edge is the least expensive—and often the most satisfying—option you have for outlining your garden bed or lawn.
- Respade your edge as necessary to keep it looking perfect.

BRICK EDGE

- Many stone edgings work best when built with a deep, long footing that keeps them from moving during winter's freeze/thaw cycles.
- You can set them deeper by placing them on edge.

COBBLESTONE EDGE

- A low boxwood hedge edges a formal garden, underscored by the strip of flat fieldstone at its base.

PRECUT STONE EDGE

- Cut stone curbing marks a clear separation between the lawn and a hedge of geranium in flower.

TERRA-COTTA TILE EDGE

- Bands of river stone, edged by terra-cotta roof tiles set on edge, add an ornamental touch to the space between lawn and garden bed.

SPADED EDGE

BRICK EDGE

PRECUT BLUESTONE EDGE

COBBLESTONE EDGE

TERRA-COTTA TILE EDGE

PATHS AND

A well-designed path can lead you

on a journey of discovery through your property.

WALKWAYS

Path and Passage

Like a hallway that connects the different rooms of your house, a path through the landscape links the different destinations on your property. A formal entry walkway leads from the sidewalk to the front door; a semiformal cut-stone path joins your dining terrace to the grill area; an informal stepping-stone path links your gardens while keeping your feet dry and out of the mud; and a soft footpath defines the well-traveled route from the kitchen to the compost bin.

Depending upon its purpose, a path can be wide or narrow, straight or meandering, ramped or stepped, long or short. What's important is to make the journey through your property as interesting as the destination itself.

above · A brick and concrete path winds its way through a sprightly garden to the front door. The picket fence divides the deep front yard into two, making the garden journey feel longer and more interesting.

left · A path of flat fieldstones provides an easy-care route to the back door for a young family.

facing page · Brick pavers link driveway to front entryway through a welcoming gardenscape. Despite a thick wall and privacy hedge, the open gate beckons a visitor to enter.

FORMAL PATHS

Without a paved walkway underfoot, we would track mud and debris right into the house. Choosing a walkway surface that is durable, not slippery, and easy to maintain (and shovel in northern climes) is essential to moving between the parts of our property that should be easily accessible throughout the year.

A formal path delineates the best route to our front, back, side, garage, or shed door. Often built wide enough for two people to walk side by side, a front walk can be curving or straight, depending upon aesthetic preferences and the destinations that need to be linked.

Natural cut stone, brick, poured concrete, or concrete pavers are just a few of the possibilities available to homeowners when they seek to build a formal path. The choice of material can either match or contrast with the materials of the house— with the former, a sense of continuity is established and with the latter, a more dynamic landscape is created. Planting shrubs and ground covers along the sides of a formal path can soften its edges and create a lovely garden experience along the way.

top right • This poured concrete walkway edged in brick provides a fully accessible walkway that is easily shoveled in winter. Plants spilling across its surface make it look less like a sidewalk when used in a home landscape.

bottom right • Dimensional concrete pavers, available in a wide range of colors, sizes, and textures, create an inexpensive and attractive entry path to this inset front door. This particular style of paver has been tumbled so that its edges look more aged.

A Walk in the Woods

A handsome "zipper" path created of thick wedges of bluestone marries traditional materials to innovative design, thereby creating a harmonious link between a Georgian-style main house and a modern pool house. The tree trunks have been limbed up, and shade-loving ground cover perennials are planted in bands of varying shades of green, in a forested landscape both soothing and vibrant.

right · The neglected woody area behind the house did nothing to complement the traditional Georgian architecture and stately pergola.

below · Selected trees were permitted to stay, underplanted with Japanese Forest Grass (*Hakonechloa macra* 'Aureola') and ferns. The landscape design, formal yet nontraditional, suits both the main house and the modern pool house shown here.

BEFORE

SEMIFORMAL PATHS

Semiformal paths are useful when we want to keep our feet dry but don't need a continuous surface underfoot to do so. Cut stone or dimensional concrete pavers, separated by gravel, plantings, or grass, offer a less formal way to link house to garden or different parts of the garden to each other and can be fun to design and to use.

Depending upon your manner of walking, you might choose bigger or smaller stones and then space them so that it's easy to walk at a normal gait. Because the pavers are cut (usually into a square or rectangular shape), make sure that you place them so that they visually relate to the geometry of the main house.

above • Square pavers zigzag through a leafy shade garden to meet a back porch.

left • A simple, shingled house looks just right with a curving semiformal path to its front door.

facing page • The kitchen entrance of this contemporary concrete house is reached by a handsome path of cut bluestone rectangles, punctuated with squares placed point to point like a diamond. Lush plantings, including grapeleaf anemone (*Anemone tomentosa* 'Robustissima') and coral bells (*Heuchera villosa* 'Autumn Bride' *and H.* 'Citronelle') flourish.

Colorful Crossroads

Two contrasting paths create a distinct hierarchy in this small front yard designed by Banyon Tree Design Studio. The formal concrete cobble path leads directly from the street entrance to the dwelling's front door in a nearly straight line. The second, smaller stepping-stone path winds informally on a journey from the driveway through abundant colorful planting beds, around a water feature, and across the main path to a flagstone breakfast patio.

The rectilinear pattern of the formal front path nicely matches the symmetrical, "all-lined-up" details of the open woodwork gate, the iron railings on the front steps, and the Craftsman-style front door. The flagstone steps of the curvilinear path invite frequent pauses to appreciate the details of the garden.

below • The water feature was installed not only for aesthetic pleasure but also to reduce noise from the street. The stepping stones, interplanted with woolly thyme (*Thymus lanuginosus*), meander romantically around the water feature, with pauses to examine the interesting foliage of rosemary, heather, and a variety of grasses.

above • The formal path takes you straight to the front door, but the curving path brings you to restful destinations, such as this breakfast patio nestled among lush planting beds.

left • The homeowner, an avid gardener, installed an abundance of his favorite plants in colors that complement the cream and sage tones of the house. Some, like the purple smokebush (*Cotinus coggygria*), provide vivid and pleasing contrasts.

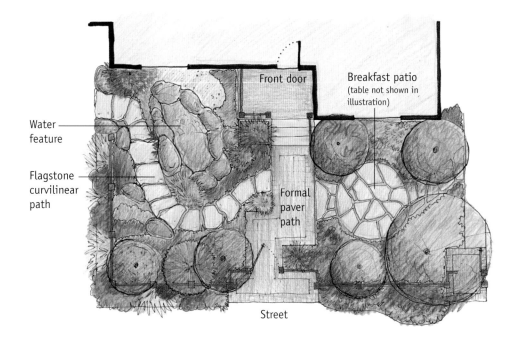

Front door

Breakfast patio
(table not shown in illustration)

Water feature

Flagstone curvilinear path

Formal paver path

Street

INFORMAL PATHS

Sometimes we want a simple way to move from one place to the other that offers an individual contemplative experience as we do so. Stepping stones, like natural-cleft flat fieldstones or quarried granite or limestone, are easy to assemble and fun to follow. Spaced several inches apart, and often sized to fit an average foot, each stepping stone should be placed the way you walk: right foot/left foot/right foot/pause. For ease of maintenance, sink each stone into a low ground cover or a lawn, so that a machine can easily mow right over them.

above • A carpet of pink ajuga (*Ajuga reptans* 'Burgundy Glow') makes this stepping stone path experience special. One rule is to space 18-in. stones about 2 in. to 3 in. apart in a slightly staggered pattern to make strolling easy.

above • These flat fieldstones follow a slight curve that leads the eye—and feet—into the garden.

above • Both the natural and quarried version of Pennsylvania bluestone are used to handsome effect in this garden. The cut bluestone walkway edged by granite gives way to a flat fieldstone path.

This informal path of Vermont schist links driveway to house through a river-like lawn. Intersperse smaller stones with large ones to enable people to plant both feet, pause, and look ahead to their destination.

SOFT PATHS

Not all paths need to be paved. Sometimes merely mowing a way through a wildflower meadow or repeatedly tramping a trail through the woods is enough to link areas of our landscape. A soft path offers an inexpensive, easy-care choice for busy homeowners on properties large and small. Good alternatives include grass, bark mulch, pine needles, stabilized soil, and pea gravel. New "steppable" ground covers are also available, but for occasional use only.

top right · In this tropical wonderland, gravel paths unite outdoor rooms into a cohesive design. The tall plants make the paths feel almost like corridors.

bottom right · Stone steps create a narrow trail through a hillside of ground covers.

below · Crunchy gravel underfoot makes for an inexpensive and permeable path material. Make sure to install a filter fabric under the gravel to keep weeds down.

right · A meditative labyrinth is created by using a ground-covering Sedum, river stones, and tamped, raked earth.

below · A mown path curves through a wildflower meadow of daisies and coreopsis, enticing us to sit awhile before following.

Path Materials

Depending upon your needs and your budget, a path can be an inexpensive or costly element in your landscape. Here is a glossary of materials and their relative costs to help you decide.

BARK MULCH
$

- Soft and quiet underfoot
- Biodegradable material; should be refreshed with new mulch each year
- Very easy to install

TAMPED EARTH
$-$$

- Permeable, yet stays firm
- Does not biodegrade but may need refreshing as soil erodes
- Often looks best with edging

PEASTONE
$$

- Permeable surface and comes in a variety of colors
- Easy to transport into small areas
- Stones may travel into garden, so use an edge to retain it

SQUARE-CUT SLABS
$$$

- Long-lasting material; comes in a variety of colors
- Easy to sweep and shovel; appropriate for a main walkway

PRECAST PAVERS
$$$

- Widely available, durable, and easy to install with tight joints
- Pavers come in a variety of patterns, colors, and textures

BRICK
$$$-$$$$

- Very widely available, durable, easy to install
- Small size allows flexibility in creating curves and patterns

BARK MULCH

TAMPED EARTH

PEASTONE

PRECAST PAVERS

SQUARE-CUT SLABS

BRICK

Steps and Stairs

Inside the house, we usually move efficiently and quickly between floors. Outside, people move up and down the landscape at a slower pace. Inclement weather brings safety concerns in the out-of-doors, so steps and staircases need to be built differently than their counterparts indoors. The rule for landscape steps is to create longer treads (14 in. as opposed to the 11 in. to 12 in. indoors) and lower risers (5 in. to 6 in., as opposed to 7½ in. indoors) to accommodate these concerns. Professionals use the following formula: Riser plus tread equals 19 in.

top right · Brightly colored tile directs the eye to a riser along this concrete paver path.

bottom right · A stone can function as both riser and tread.

below · A short stairway between driveway and lawn is made of long narrow treads set on stacked-stone risers.

'Baby Tears' (*Soleirolia soleirolii*) grows in the grouted spaces between slates on this long garden staircase.

LANDINGS

Landings give us a place to pause as we move up
and down the different areas of our property. They
are particularly important to break up a long run
of stairs so that we may catch our breath and look
ahead to the next landing. Make them deeper,
wider, or another shape to set them apart from
the path.

top right • These thick granite steps form both tread and riser,
while retaining the gravel landings that occur periodically
along this long outdoor staircase.

bottom right • A handrail and a landing provide security to
anyone using these front steps, whatever the weather.

below • This sandstone landing doubles as a terrace sized just
for two.

Landings at each slight turn in the path break up a long staircase on this steep terraced slope. Each bluestone step has been split along the top with a rougher rock face as the riser.

Bridges

A bridge is a structure that allows passage across a barrier or a gap. Often built of wood or steel, many times it crosses a valley, ravine, or stream, linking one shore to the other. Like a tunnel, which burrows through an obstacle rather than over it, a bridge is a continuation of a path where it otherwise might not be able to go.

facing page, top • Stepping stones raised high above a "sea" of gravel act like a bridge across water. Japanese maple leaves remind us of the passing of the seasons.

facing page, bottom • These wide planks of wood are set in a staggered pattern, allowing passage across a sunken garden of birch trees underplanted with ferns.

above • A wooden bridge spans a babbling brook. The arcing handrails echo the pleasing curve underfoot.

right • A bridge extends over an elegant dry streambed, which also serves as a drain for runoff in this yard.

PLANTINGS

Hardscapes are brought to life when you plant trees, shrubs, ground covers,

and vines, as well as flowering perennials and annuals.

And don't forget those edibles.

Planting Schemes

Design professionals divide landscape elements into two parts: hardscapes—the decks, walls, paths, terraces, and driveways that are permanent features of our property—and softscapes—the trees, shrubs, vines, flowers, and ground covers that live and change throughout the seasons and over the years. These softscape plants are the easiest and often least expensive way to make a quick and dramatic change to your landscape.

From a stately collection of trees to a vivid explosion of perennial plantings, plants can completely alter the character of your outdoor space. Providing utilitarian solutions for a wide range of design challenges, plants provide screening, surface water collection, wildlife habitat, and ground cover. Last but certainly not least, plants supply sustenance and satisfaction when we try our hand at growing our own food.

Plants are dynamic, changing through the seasons and over the years; they provide energy and excitement in the landscape. While a large boulder may stay in its place for many years, the same is not necessarily so for a plant. Most plants can be easily moved around. Shrubs can be reshaped or moved if need be, and even mature trees can be cut down and perennial beds can be reworked as often as necessary. Plants are the most malleable part of the landscape.

New gardeners benefit from starting small and investing in their own plant education. Careful observation can go a long way. Novices can learn a lot by keeping records of bloom times or by visiting other gardens to take notes on successful plant combinations. Or hire a gardening coach, join a gardening club, or work one-on-one with a professional designer for the first few years.

above • Trees provide a sense of formality as in this allée of hornbeams (*Carpinus fastigiata*). Their graceful forms lead the eye down a perfectly symmetrical approach to a traditional-style home.

above • The informal asymmetry of these beds lends a rustic appeal to this entryway.

Island beds break up the space in this patio, creating rooms and passageways in what would otherwise have been an unbroken expanse of stone.

Bed Layouts

The shape of your beds sets the stage for your plantings. It also expresses the style of your garden. Whether they are symmetrically aligned or organically shaped, formal or natural, the beds will be most cohesive if they relate to the surrounding landscape and existing architecture.

Be sure beds are deep enough to plant in layers that ascend in height from front to back. Remember that beds of flowering shrubs and perennials provide the solid form that gives shape to the adjacent lawn.

above • In this imaginative design, "islands" of clover provide visual interest in a sea of grass—and forage for one contented sheep.

This colorful sweep of layered plantings creates a harbor around an open lawn.

Dense plantings in this small backyard make the space seem larger. Both the deck and the small seating area under the arbor feel enfolded by the lush garden.

Rain Garden

A rain garden is a beautiful way to solve the persistent problem of surface water run-off. Because more and more of the earth's surface is being paved or covered with human-made structures, the soil can't do its essential job of recycling rainwater. Instead, the water runs off all those paved surfaces—picking up contaminants such as oil, fertilizer, pesticides, and other pollutants as it goes—and carries it all to the nearest waterway or sewer drain.

You can keep rainwater out of overworked sewer systems and help prevent the pollution of our lakes and rivers. Direct the rainwater that lands on impervious surfaces like roofs and driveways to a planted filtration basin right on your property. Deep-rooted plants use the water, and a healthy bed of soil with all of its microscopic organisms will break down harmful contaminants.

Rain gardens are a great place to use native plants, which evolved to fare well in your area without fertilizers and pesticides that would impede microbial activity in the soil and contaminate the rainwater.

top right · The stone streambed was installed on both sides of the existing mortared flagstone path to divert water into a culvert, with buried PVC pipe to carry water underneath the path's concrete base.

bottom right · This attractive project was actually fairly low-budget because the design worked with, not against, the existing features of the landscape. The culvert, visible at the back, was incorporated into the design with added boulders and plantings.

facing page · Turning a problem into an asset: heavy rains frequently converted this Bethesda, Md., house's downward-sloping front yard into a raging river. The rain garden design created by Melissa Clark made use of an existing swale and massive onsite boulders to form a landscape that can stand up to periodic flooding—beautifully.

Trees

Trees lend structure to the landscape. They provide shade, verticality, screening, and beauty. Whether deciduous or evergreen, trees are stable forms in the garden year-round. Living for decades or even centuries, they are long-lasting legacies in the landscapes we create.

Trees are an essential component of our outdoor spaces, often fostering a feeling of comfort and a sense of place, although it needn't take a grove or a forest to make people feel at home. Many plains and southwestern states have a natural scarcity of trees. In climates like these, carefully selected specimen trees can make a strong statement.

Above most other landscape elements, trees have the power to subdue the imposition of human-made architecture. Offering height, structural stability, and visual mass, trees can help to "settle" a built structure into its natural surroundings. Often the beauty and value of a neighborhood dwelling is related to the age and appropriateness of its trees.

Since trees can be such a prominent feature in the garden, their species, size, style, care, and placement should be carefully considered. Natural or habitat gardens benefit both visually and functionally from a selection of native tree species. Trees with dependable, symmetrical habits are the best choices for formal spaces. Flowering species often fit well into ornamental gardens. Evergreens are the best option for year-round screening.

right • The tall slender trunk of this evergreen tree is duplicated in the older specimen that grows along the fence line. Older trees bring prominence and venerability to a property.

above · This clean-lined, geometrically arranged space might seem too rigid without the charming presence of this mature hydrangea (*Hydrangea paniculata*) tree. With its soft, low arching canopy and slender, delicate branches, the tree sits at the juncture between two terraces, enlivening and connecting the spaces.

left · When siting trees, think of the future—a mature tree can not only frame views from the house, but, when sited correctly, will provide cooling shade from the summer sun, a natural air-conditioner.

STRUCTURE

Trees can act as a living wall to screen, frame, or emphasize views. They can serve as an alternate or complement to walls or fences, offering softness, variability, seasonal color, and beauty. Evergreen trees certainly provide the most consistent visual barrier, but combinations involving fences, climbers, shrubs, and deciduous trees can provide multiple layers of visual interest.

right • Fastigiate trees are narrow, upright specimens that are selected for their erect branches that taper toward the top. Three Ginkgo trees sit prominently in front of this contemporary home, mediating between architecture and natural landscape.

below • In this scenario, it is obvious that the designer chose to retain and showcase this elegant tree. This decision drove the placement of the walkway in an elegant arc around the tree's canopy. In the process, the planting bed took shape. Note the highlights of color-coordinated annuals that emphasize the tree.

Crab apple trees frame this garden entrance and provide partial screening for the private garden within.

PRIVACY

Trees also provide an inexpensive way to achieve privacy for your property, whether designed as vertical screening between properties, a hedged garden room near the house, or set off as a stand on their own. Planting tall evergreens close together provides a nearly impenetrable partition and creates the greatest sense of privacy, but also can cast the deepest shadows.

Deciduous trees can be planted in rows for a leafy aerial hedge or as a loose grove whose thick planting depth blocks out undesired views. When you mix the foliage of deciduous and evergreen trees together, along with shrubs layered at their base, you create not only a handsome privacy screen but also an elegant woodland garden at the edge of your property. A stand of palm trees or bamboo planted along the perimeter of your landscape is another quick way to gain a sense of seclusion, but make sure you erect a sturdy in-ground barrier to keep the plants where they're welcome and out of the rest of your garden. Of course, the larger the specimen you plant, the more quickly you'll achieve the privacy that you're seeking.

top right • As tall and robust as the building itself, these columnar evergreen trees create a third architectural wall in this courtyard.

bottom right • With a brick wall, shrubs, multistemmed trees, and a vine-covered fence, this landscape offers an interesting, multilayered screen from unwanted views.

facing page • Trees come in all shapes and sizes. These palms form a tight screen and offer complete privacy to this outdoor living space.

Inside Tropical Retreat

When we look inside the fence of the Seattle garden discussed in the first chapter on p. 15, we find a paradise of palms, grasses, and bamboos, all in keeping with the tropical theme created by Banyon Tree Design Studio.

The dense planting of tropical shrubs offers complete screening and creates the illusion of wildness in this residential setting. The path is carved from the jungle and the flowers are colorful surprises, decorating the way. The designer invites travelers to pause along the path with destination spaces that contain diversions and places to sit and enjoy the view.

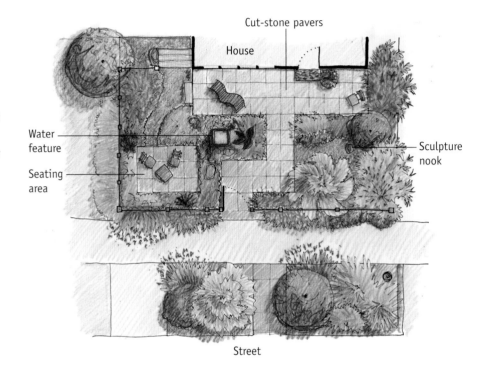

Cut-stone pavers

House

Water feature

Seating area

Sculpture nook

Street

left • There is no reason why the route to the front door need be direct. Adding sharp, geometric corners to this path has lengthened the journey from point A to B, stretching a short trip into a larger experience.

facing page • Areca palms (*Dypsis lutescens*) arch over the sculpture of a face, while rivers of pebbles and beach stone sweep into and out of the cut-stone patio. All around are artfully placed plantings that rise out of a ground cover of baby tears (*Soleirolia soleirolii*).

COLOR

Green is just one of the many colors of trees. Blooms and fall foliage aside, the spectrum of available leaf colors is as broad as the rainbow. Many cultivars are specifically bred for color intensity. Japanese maples (such as *Acer palmatum* 'Bloodgood') are known for their rich red leaves. False cypress (*Chamaecyparis lawsoniana* 'Lutea') needles are an electric yellow throughout the season. Skyrocket juniper (*Juniperus scopulorum* 'Skyrocket') cools the color palette with tones of frosty blue. The Rohani copper beech (*Fagus sylvatica* 'Rohanii') is a stately tree with purple foliage.

above • Autumn can bring a whole new color palette into the garden. Remember to keep fall foliage in mind when coordinating with surrounding painted surfaces and blooming perennials.

right • This newly planted redbud tree (*Cercis canadensis* 'Forest Pansy') spreads wide its delicate branches etched in tiny magenta flowers to veil a staircase of cantilevered concrete treads, suspended as if by magic above the ground.

facing page, top • The heritage birch (*Betulus nigra* 'Heritage') has unique, exfoliating bark in warm cream and orange tones.

facing page, bottom • The blues of these spruces provide contrast to the greens and warm tones of the perennials. Additional blue-toned perennials like catmint (*Nepeta*) or Russian sage (*Perovskia*) could strengthen the visual relationship.

Shrubs

All perennial borders can benefit from the addition of shrubs. Having slower growth and less seasonal variability than herbaceous perennials, they provide shape and structure to a garden even in its dormancy. Evergreen shrubs such as dwarf blue spruce (*Picea pungens*) and those with winter interest such as winterberry (*Ilex verticillata*) will provide color and structure to a garden even in the off-season months.

Shrubs are the bridge between ground-level plants and trees. They are transitional elements that help mediate the differences among plantings of various sizes. Often requiring less seasonal care than many herbaceous perennials, shrubs are good entry-level plants for the new gardener or low-maintenance garden.

FOLIAGE AND COLOR

Just as with trees, shrubs can be found in a variety of foliage hues. Even the color green has countless variations. Placing colorful shrubs in the perennial border can have a bold effect, so it is important to coordinate the colors of shrubs and perennials' flowers and foliage. For example, the purple hues of the leaves of the smoke bush (*Cotinus coggygria* 'Royal Purple') can be augmented by hints of purple in the garden, such as purple-leaved cimicifuga (*Actaea racemosa* 'Brunette') or Joe Pye weed (*Eutrochium purpureum* 'Chocolate'). Ninebark (*Physocarpus opulifolius* 'Coppertina') is a deep russet-orange, which can look striking against a ground cover of chartreuse-leaved hostas or Euphorbia.

above • The actual blooms of this garden are limited but the color is vivid. The designer has created a complex expression using a simple palette of varied color, contrasting texture, and undulating form.

above • Another play on color, this garden uses a narrow spectrum of hues but relies heavily on shape and form to create a tasteful composition. The boxwood hedge provides a border for a tapestry of plants of alternating tints. The result is a formal, controlled, and stately collection of greens.

FLOWERING

Like herbaceous perennials, many shrubs are bred
for the splendor and color of their blooms. Some species have countless cultivars offering slight variations
of color, height, flower size, hardiness, or bloom time.
Generally speaking, flowering shrubs require much less
maintenance than the average herbaceous perennial
and are therefore a good way to get a display of flowers
without the time commitment of a perennial garden.

right · Hydrangea cultivars are plentiful, offering a huge range of
bloom times from spring until fall.

below · This naturalized collection of azaleas offers breathtaking
spring bloom—and the foliage remains neat and attractive when
the flowering season is over.

Climbers

Climbing vines rise skyward, above the cluttered zone of plant competition. Some climbers sprawl informally over telephone poles or clamber into nearby trees; others need to be trained to mount a formal structure such as an arbor or a pergola.

Different types of vines have varying inclinations and growth habits. Some climbers, like roses and grapevines, have woody stems that remain year-round, even in the winter. Others, like some types of clematis, produce new growth from the ground each year so they have a season of dormancy during which they might not be visible—or they might remain as an unsightly tangle of bare vines. Be sure to choose carefully which type of climber you place at your front entry to avoid an unsightly mess in the off-season.

Vines can climb in a variety of ways. Twining vines like wisteria send out shoots that encircle a support. Grapes and sweet peas twist their delicate tendrils around close-by supports to keep climbing. Other plants, like climbing roses, use their thorns to hold onto a support, while plants like ivy employ little rootlets to cling to the side of a house. Learning the growth habits of your climbing vines helps you to know how best to support them as they wind their way up toward the sky.

top right • Annual climbers can be planted in pots and changed from year to year.

bottom right • Clematis come in many colors and bloom times. Here, two complementary varieties of this vigorous vine nearly cover a birdhouse structure, a charming sight in spring and summer.

Grapevines cast a dappled shade, providing shelter from the sun and creating a rustic, romantic hideaway.

Perennials

Perennials are the workhorses of the traditional flower garden. Their ability to survive the winter in dormancy is what distinguishes them from annuals.

Herbaceous perennials have soft stems that die back to the ground every year. Phlox, Shasta daisies, beebalm, and irises are types of herbaceous perennials. Offering changing seasons of bloom and form, they constantly transform your garden landscape throughout the growing season.

Perennials are perhaps the trickiest plants with which to work in the garden. Gardeners should become familiar with the plants' height, color, shape, habit, season of bloom, and short- and long-term maintenance. A successful garden blends and balances the varied look and temperaments of multiple plants into a working composition. If you're a beginner, don't be intimidated; gardeners old and new balance experience with trial and error. A perennial bed is always evolving. Don't be afraid to move your plants to new locations as you get to know them.

top right · To create a meadow in your backyard, you can either seed or plant perennial wildflowers (as plug plants or seedlings) for a more instant effect. Here, lupines combine with daisies to create a delightful tangle.

bottom right · This grassy lane invites us to stop and smell the blossoms along the way.

facing page, bottom · This complex multileveled garden shows good understanding of plant height and habit. The back of the border features taller screening shrubs in the 8-ft. to 10-ft. range, the middle showcases larger perennials and lower shrubs in the 4-ft. to 7-ft. range, and planted at the front of the border are smaller annuals and perennials.

Meet Your Neighbors

Every garden, large or small, can provide habitat for some of the world's creatures. Get to know the flora and fauna that are native to where you live and try to incorporate them into your garden design whenever possible. The beautiful flowers of the butterfly bush (Buddleia) are well-known to attract butterflies—but many people don't realize that they do not provide any food for the insects' larvae. For many ornamental garden plants, there are attractive native plant alternatives that will provide food and habitat. Insects not only help to pollinate our flowers and fruit—they are also an irreplaceable food source for songbirds and other creatures.

Grasses

Grasses are low-maintenance plants that work well in natural landscapes. Filling large spaces and small, there are ornamental grasses appropriate for a wide variety of landscape settings in a subtle range of color options. Sedge (*Carex*) varieties tend to be shade-tolerant, moisture-loving, and under 24 in. in height. Several species of Miscanthus, however, can reach more than 10 ft. tall and are happiest in low-nutrient soils in full sun.

above • Whereas turf lawns are the traditional popular fallback, gardeners are now turning to more ecologically appropriate ornamental grasses to fill large neutral spaces.

top right • Grasses also bloom; their flowers are referred to as inflorescences.

bottom right • Fall is when grasses really shine. Black-eyed Susan (*Rudbeckia fulgida* 'Goldsturm') and firetail mountain fleece (*Persicaria amplexicaulis* 'Firetail') are good companion plants for many small grasses like this sapphire blue oat grass (*Helictotrichon sempervirens* 'Saphirsprudel').

Grasses line this walkway, creating the impression of a streambed. Russian sage (*Perovskia atriplicifolia*) rounds the bend near the path's outlet. Blending well with the grasses' flowing, informal nature, the sage offers just a hint of subtle color to the mix.

Ground covers

Bare ground is difficult to maintain and has no real ecological benefits. Ground covers are earth carpets that provide weed protection, prevent surface run-off, diversify habitats, and enhance the beauty of the groundscape.

Contemporary gardeners are leaning away from ground covers like lawn grass that require a high degree of maintenance and lots of fertilizer and water to sustain. Instead, ground covers can act like a living mulch that can help retain moisture and eliminate the need for weeding. They are an effective way to add large swaths of color, texture, interest, or unity to the garden setting.

above • Chartreuse hostas, the red-tinged foliage of astilbes, and purple-flowering bugleweed (*Ajuga reptans*) add color and variety to a soft carpeting of ferns. All of these plants spread quickly to cover bare spaces in the garden.

left • Pink dianthus (*Dianthus gratianopolitanus* 'Mountain Mist') makes a soft, low border to a perennial garden.

facing page • These Virginia bluebells (*Mertensia virginica*) are ephemeral, meaning that after blooming they will wither back to ground level and go dormant. Their ground cover effect is limited to the spring.

GREEN ROOFS

A vegetative layer grown on a rooftop, called a green roof, helps reduce run-off and increases on-site absorption of rain. Green roofs also can reduce heating and cooling costs—especially in warmer climates. Depending upon a roof's load capacity, perennials, herbs, grasses, and even vegetables can be planted in a growing medium over a waterproof membrane.

right · Succulents like Sedum or Sempervivum can be beautifully diverse and ornamental in nature and are excellent choices for the roof garden. Their varied forms create a living tapestry.

below · This ingenious green roof design not only catches water to sustain a surface garden but also has an overflow that diverts it to a garden below.

The plantings on the roof of this simple yet elegant outbuilding share a color palette with the plants along the path—an effective strategy for anchoring the structure in the landscape.

Annuals

Nothing packs a punch like annual flowers. Annuals, by definition, survive only one season and are often used to supplement and extend blooming times, fill holes created by ephemerals, conceal the dying foliage of bulbs, or simply bring new color to the landscape.

Many annuals grow an astonishing amount during their single season. A tiny angel's trumpet (*Datura inoxia*) purchased at the garden center in May might be 3 ft. tall and 5 ft. wide by August. Be sure to learn the eventual size and growth habits of the annuals you choose—and look for new and unusual varieties. It's fun and easy to experiment with plants that will last only a year. Just be sure to give them plenty of compost or fertilizer, and observe their sun and moisture requirements.

above • This collection of snapdragons (*Antirrhinum*) is virtually bursting with bloom and color. A trellis supports annual sweet peas (*Lathyrus odoratus*), whose old-fashioned fragrance makes them a cottage-garden favorite.

left • These glorious golden poppies (*Eschscholzia californica*), ubiquitous in California and other western states, are perennials in their native regions but annuals in colder zones where they are killed by frost. Other tender perennials that cold-climate gardeners can use as annuals include impatiens, begonias, and pelargoniums (commonly called geraniums).

Annuals can provide reliable color that lasts throughout the summer season. Placing them in containers around a seating area lets you alter an outdoor room the way you might change slipcovers or table linens indoors.

Containers

As architectural accents in the garden, planted containers lend focal interest to your outdoor landscapes. Pots also keep planting soil off patios and decks while providing a place to feature brightly colored annuals or specimen plants. For cold-climate gardeners, containers are an excellent home for citrus trees and other exotics that look lovely on a terrace in summer but need to come indoors for the winter.

These days, containers come in a variety of materials and finishes. Traditional clay, light resin, stone, metal, or concrete pots bring a vast range of styles, colors, and textures to our gardens.

right • Tall planters create a frame for this entrance. Their color and form complement the architecture.

below • Containers can offer boundaries to control vigorous spreaders like these colonizing strawberry plants.

Airy papyrus plant (*Cyperus papyrus*) arches gracefully above plantings of purple-leaved and variegated coleus (*Solenostemon*), sweet potato vines (*Ipomoea batatas*) in lime green and nearly black, and flowering lantana and petunias. Planters color-coordinated with the wall and terrace pavers allow the plants to stand out.

Potted Plants

Buy new, reuse a barrel or a tray, or make your own—
pots, alone or in groupings, are a wonderful way to bring
plants into every corner of your life.

1. Not everyone has room for a vegetable garden, but a patio planting is mobile and can fit into the smallest of spaces. 2. This handsome container, the inverted form of the stone column beside it, holds a colorful collection of shade-tolerant annuals. 3. Even northern gardens can feature cacti and other non-native succulents when planted in pots. 4. Succulent arrangements make wonderful centerpieces on an outdoor table. 5. This tower shelf is an attractive display for a large collection of potted tender succulents in the summer months. In winter, it is brought inside to avoid the killing frosts.

Edibles

For reasons as diverse as thrift, taste, and ecology, more and more people are learning to grow food in their own backyard. Known to some as modern homesteading, this gardening tradition is reshaping the way we live and interact with our own landscapes. For some, this may mean a few tomato plants in a pot on a patio. Others may indulge in a 1-acre vegetable plot and a flock of free-range chickens. Whatever the level and motivation, people are finding the edible garden to be one of the most satisfying ways to spend time on their land.

above • Many people don't recognize full-grown asparagus, which becomes a tall, feathery plant after harvest: a delicious spring treat followed by a beautiful privacy screen.

facing page, bottom · An edible garden can have a beautiful and organized, yet informal charm. In this design, utilitarian features are also ornamental: a rustic fence keeps the critters out, while tepees that support runner beans are painted a cheerful cobalt blue. Make sure to include seating, as this gardener did, to ensure that you'll take time to enjoy the view.

right · City dwellers can plant an entire garden in pots. Herbs are easily brought in to spend the winter months on a windowsill. Be sure to refresh the soil for each new occupant, as nutrients are quickly depleted by the demands of annual vegetables, and soil can also harbor disease and pests.

below · The edible garden can also fit into a formal garden plan. Here, a traditional parterre design features precisely edged grass paths and tightly controlled symmetrical plantings of thriving vegetables.

Pack 'Em In

Marilee Kuhlmann made the most of every square foot of her front yard and southern California climate to grow everything from capers to jujubes. Redwood raised beds are full of salad greens and other vegetables, while artichoke plants spread their prehistoric-looking fronds along the sidewalk. Even vertical space was pressed into use, with flowerpots wired to the fencing and espaliered fruit trees hugging the walls. Figs are trained over an archway, and beans twine up a metal obelisk. The wire fencing accommodates climbing plants such as grapevines, and swallowtail butterflies, attracted by the fennel and parsley, love to attach their chrysalises to the wire. Interplanted throughout are perennial herbs and plants that attract beneficial pollinators, such as yarrow, lavender, lemon verbena, and various salvias.

right • There is always room for a small tree in the carefully planned vegetable garden. This kumquat tree offers visual punctuation to the bed's end. Vigorous planting of strawberries and chard are controlled by containers and edging.

below • Fragrant perennial herbs like this rosemary are good plantings to grace an entry.

facing page • A place for everything and everything in its place . . . a well-organized vegetable garden like this one is easier to maintain. The garden hose hanging neatly in a central location is proof of thoughtful planning.

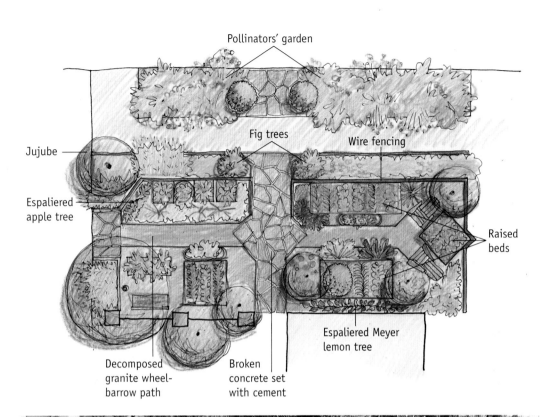

Pollinators' garden

Jujube

Fig trees

Wire fencing

Espaliered
apple tree

Raised
beds

Decomposed
granite wheel-
barrow path

Broken
concrete set
with cement

Espaliered Meyer
lemon tree

Greenhouses

Greenhouses are elegant additions to the modern homestead. A place to start annuals or harbor tender plants, the greenhouse is a valuable tool to extend the growing season. Greenhouses are also important architectural features of the landscape, and their style, placement, and incorporation will impact the way the garden is viewed as a whole.

If you long to garden year-round, there are many greenhouse kits to fit your style, gardening needs, and budget. You can choose frames of wood, steel, or aluminum, with walls or windows of glass or polycarbonite. If you're handy, try making a frame around some old windows to build a cold frame or glass house yourself.

above • Brick knee walls hold in heat and provide a solid backdrop for potting benches. Crankable windows at the peak are important to vent the hot air that rises when the sun pours in the glass walls and roof.

left • A cold frame fits snugly in the corner of this courtyard vegetable garden and provides a place for tender vegetable seedlings to stay warm before being transplanted into the beds and pots.

Pest Control

What about the bugs? A diversified ecosystem is a healthy one. There are always bugs in the garden environment, and they play a role in the lifecycle of plants. Whether it be in the pollination of flowers or decomposition of old organic material, insects have beneficial functions. Certainly there are the undesirables (like squash bugs) and invasive species (like Japanese beetles) that plague us. For these, row covers, preventative biological controls, and hand picking may be the best ways to rid your garden of the unwanted. Chickens are good at seeking out nymph-stage insects and may be used to control pests.

Not all greenhouses need be elaborate or custom-made. This repurposed cottage with its south-facing window serves as a rustic greenhouse and blends perfectly with the surrounding architecture.

DETAILS

Crafting the details of your landscape

IN THE

links inside to outside and brings focus to the whole property.

LANDSCAPE

Delighting in the Details

Look around your house—what is it that most catches your eye? Often it's the little details—the pictures on the wall, the accent colors on the pillows, the hanging chandelier, the favorite vase filled with flowers—that enliven and personalize a space and bring delight to you and your friends and family. Similarly, it's the details you place outside that add a layer of finish and sparkle to the landscape around your house. Selecting and placing appropriate focal points—including fire and water elements—ornament, and lighting all enhance our enjoyment of home outside.

The special decorative objects that add an embellishing note to our homes enhance our enjoyment of our property. Some of us prefer choosing one-of-a-kind pieces that stand alone in the landscape; others enjoy making and displaying collections and placing them in just the right locations. Just as we decorate the inside of our homes with special knick-knacks or seasonal ornaments, so too can we adorn our landscapes with beloved objects—the details that catch the eye and make us smile.

top right • Like having a Christmas tree in your backyard year-round, this collection of blue bottles and gourds decorates the branches of a small ornamental tree.

bottom right • A sculpture need not be elevated to capture attention. Here, a stone head appearing unexpectedly at ground level draws the eye to the striking and varied foliage of nearby plantings.

facing page • Light picks up the color and texture of the slender stalks and seed head of this papyrus plant, creating a tall, ethereal focal point that contrasts with a squat Japanese lantern.

Focal Points

When a landscape is designed around a focal point, it tends to draw us in and hold our attention. Focal points are the objects in a landscape that catch our eyes, like a central sculpture, a distant view, or a bubbling fountain. Focal points may be tiny or overscale, viewed close up or in the distance, in motion or not. A well-placed focal point can be the centerpiece of a whole landscape.

A frame around a painting creates a clear border that surrounds and highlights the image within. Similarly, each window in our house can act as a frame that makes a picture out of the landscape in our view. We can also use elements of architecture, like porch posts or gateways, to define the edges of a scene and thereby draw the eye. The space between two tree trunks forms a natural frame around the setting sun at dusk. When we find or create a frame around a focal object—by placing a pedestal beneath a sculpture, a moongate that frames a specimen tree, or a pergola that delineates the clouds in the sky, the frame expands our normal view of the landscape around us and makes it special.

top right • An unusual bronze sculpture occupies the corner of this verdant garden's patio. Is it a chaise longue, a focal point, or both?

bottom right • A number of elements contribute to the framing effect in this design: the neatly trimmed hedges approaching the bench, the round potted boxwoods flanking it (and echoing the shape of the ornamental ball), and the rose-decked arching trellis overhead. In a playful twist reminiscent of a Dutch painting, a framed mirror reflects it all back to the viewer.

facing page • The white painted posts create an opening in this latticework fence, framing a compelling vista of a limbed-up tree and stone wall that further frame the seascape beyond.

Dynamic Focal Points

Focal points in the landscape catch the eye when forces of nature animate them. The sparkle of flowing water, the movement of wind chimes, the flitting of birds at a feeder—these are just a few of the many ways that actual movement brings focal objects to life. Another way is to find or create sculptures that feel as though they're in motion and place them in your garden.

1. Wind chimes bring movement and sound into this colorful outdoor table setting. 2. Shadows cast by the feathery foliage of papyrus plants animate the stucco wall behind this outdoor sofa. 3. A tiny painted birdhouse placed on a stake anywhere in the garden adds a complementary accent of color and draws attention (and feathered friends) to a favorite corner. 4. Multicolored blown-glass sculptures look like overscale flowers sprouting through the deep green leaves of this shade garden. 5. A long, low channel of water, known as a rill, riffles through beach stones and pours into a ferny pool below.

STONE

Used correctly, stones can act as both focal point and the backbone of any landscape. They appear more natural when they seem to emerge from deep within the ground and are set in odd pairings or sets of threes, fives, and sevens. While stones set vertically more easily grab our attention, those that are placed parallel and low to the ground feel restful, as though they've always been there.

top right · Whenever possible, use local stone. The existing ledge is complemented with other stones from the property as a border for the driveway of this contemporary Boston-area home.

bottom right · A hillside of wildflowers cascades past a focal stone, set firmly into the earth.

below · Irregularly shaped swimming pools can look like natural ponds when edged with stones.

In this Japanese-inspired design, ornamental stones were thoughtfully placed on a geometrically arranged grid of rocks and gravel of contrasting colors and textures. Black washed river stones create a horizontal frame around the three-stone setting.

WATER

Water provides one of the best points of focus in a landscape. Moving water draws both our eyes and our ears, and often birds and other critters as well. Elaborate waterfalls and decorative backyard streams may be more than many of us have the means to create, but simple all-in-one garden fountains can add visual and aural delights on a shoestring budget.

Still water also delights the eye while cooling the atmosphere. Small lily ponds or simple birdbaths can reflect the movement in the sky and bring contemplative delight into the backyard landscape.

right • A bubbling pinecone birdbath fountain is elevated above the surrounding plantings, so its music can carry to the far corners of the garden. The owners often sit outside at night to enjoy the sound.

below • A spitting frog fountain lends a whimsical appeal to an otherwise formal rectangular pool. Lily pads floating on the water reinforce the froggy theme.

top • This limestone basin, wearing a lovely patina of use, sits atop a bed of gravel at the very center of a formal parterre, where it can be seen and heard from an adjacent seating area.

bottom • Anyone can create a water garden by using a galvanized horse trough to hold water plants. To keep the water moving and create ripples on its surface, you can aerate the plantings by adding a small bubbler.

Water Music

This lovely Vermont property, designed by Broadleaf Landscape Architecture, creates a series of gardens designed on a water theme. As visitors approach the house, they spy an oblong reflecting pool surrounded by lush plantings of daylilies, lady's mantle, spirea, and grasses. In the background, a handsome willow tree anchors the vignette while also providing a focal point for the large swimming pond below.

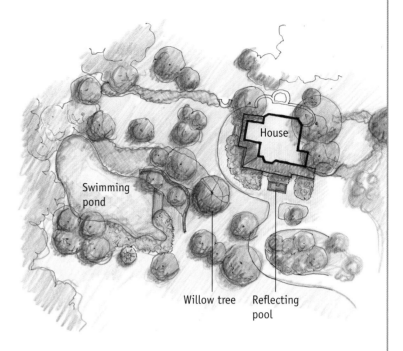

above • Bluestone coping provides a clean frame for this handsome pool planted with water lilies and lotus and animated by a spitting frog fountain. Red daylilies echo the color of the rafter tails over the long front porch of this Vermont home.

left • A long deck, nestled against a steep planted slope, sits just above the water level of the swimming pond.

left • A Corten®-steel pool rises asymmetrically from a ground cover of grasses in a grove of multistemmed trees.

below • This small infinity-edged pool reflects the shasta viburnum *(V. plicatum f. tomentosum)* and nearby forest when not in use as a swim-in-place exercise pool.

FIRE

From time immemorial, fire has been a vital part of our outdoor landscapes. Originally used for cooking and warmth, fire has increasingly become an ornamental and focal feature that draws families and friends into the landscape at night. Firepits, firebowls, fireplaces, bread and pizza ovens, and outdoor kitchens and grills—whether wood or gas-fired, all animate and bring thermal delight to our experience of the out-of-doors.

right • A gas firepit is easily turned on and off to illuminate a corner of this concrete deck.

below • This sunken firepit is constructed of concrete blocks made to look like natural stone. The thick caps on both pit and wall serve as bench or tabletop for an intimate few or a large crowd roasting marshmallows.

A theme of concrete variations sets off this fire garden as special. A diagonal carpet of blue-tinted pavers contrasts with the round firebowl, all set on a striped channel of round riverstone.

Gather around the Fire

JMMDS was asked to turn an unused side yard into an outdoor "fire garden" for a couple that likes to entertain at their Massachusetts seaside home. We created a formal path that links the new octagonal bluestone patio to an existing terrace, centering the fire pit on the owners' kitchen window. A grassy play space is edged by cut bluestone and surrounded by perennial gardens.

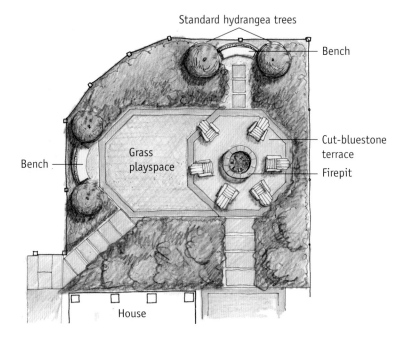

Standard hydrangea trees

Bench

Bench

Grass playspace

Cut-bluestone terrace

Firepit

House

Dancing flames draw convivial groups together and invite quiet conversations on cool summer evenings under the stars.

above • The homeowner's white curved benches offer contemplative seating framed by standard hydrangea trees that draw the eye to the edges of the space.

right • Beds of exuberant plantings, including hydrangeas, roses, geraniums, and salvia, bring color and texture to the Fire Garden.

FIREPLACES

There is no pleasure like sitting before a blazing fireplace—and it needn't be inside your house. If your dwelling lacks a fireplace or your climate makes indoor fires uncomfortably warm, you can still enjoy all the delights of a fireplace right in your garden. Outdoor fireplaces can be freestanding or built into the wall of a structure, as shown below. If you are installing a new outdoor fireplace area, be sure to hire a licensed contractor who will observe all safety precautions. Don't forget to consider convenient (and attractive) wood storage and ash removal in your design.

above • Fireplaces have made a comeback in recent years as the centerpiece of outdoor living rooms.

OUTDOOR KITCHENS

If possible, locate open-air dining spaces right next to the kitchen so carrying food between inside and out is not an impediment to eating under the stars. Where you locate the cooking space—whether in the middle of the eating/entertainment space or to the edge—will depend upon the personality of the chef.

These days, durable moveable grills, with extension arms that hold platters and grilling utensils, can be used no matter the season. Others prefer the convenience of an outdoor kitchen, complete with built-in grill, refrigerator, and even a prep sink. Because they necessitate the building of walls to house the different elements, it pays to use the services of a landscape or kitchen professional to integrate the kitchen into a full-scale landscape design.

above • This stainless steel grill was built into a fireproof nook adjacent to the dining area, making it easy for the grillmeister to bring hot food to the table without burning the house down.

right • With its roof, solid wood pillars, and doors into the house, this outdoor kitchen feels like an extension of the home. It also provides every amenity a chef could want, ensuring that no one will be stuck indoors cooking while everyone else is enjoying the party outside.

facing page • Some fireplaces can be used from either inside or outside the house. This massive stone wall with its huge sandstone mantle allows wood storage below the large firebox, with chimney above.

Furniture

With so many outdoor furniture choices on the market these days, it's tempting to buy whatever's on sale at the time. But just like inside, finding the right armchair, table, or sofa can make or break the look and feel of an open-air room. Consider harmonizing the furniture's style with that of your house and use color to match or accent the plantings around it.

top right • Teak chairs sit low down for privacy on this untreated wooden roof deck. A planter filled with ornamental grasses acts both as railing and privacy screen.

bottom right • A folding table and chairs turn a concrete patio into an outdoor café. Their lines may be delicate, but the vivid color packs a punch entirely appropriate for this tropical-themed garden.

below • Handsome outdoor furniture set on a patio of pea-stone brings living room-like comfort right into the middle of the garden.

right • Stools and ottomans can accommodate occasional guests in small spaces and during intimate gatherings are useful as footrests or side tables.

below • A teak dining set perfectly suits weathered shingles and traditional architecture. Good design, solid construction, and an unpretentious finish give an airy, beachy feel to this dining area.

BENCHES

Who doesn't love a good bench? When backed up against a tree trunk, wall, or tall plantings, a bench provides the security and comfort we often seek in an open landscape. Not only does a bench need to receive us with open arms, but it also should face toward an interesting focal point or feature. Whether stationary or swinging, we can nestle into our bench comfortably for hours, gazing out on our planted paradise.

above • This painted bench sets nicely into a nook designed just to fit. Note how the paving pattern echoes the interlocking curve pattern on its back.

above • This old teak bench gets a second life as a reading nook when painted a fun color and set right into the garden.

above • This large bench becomes both protective wall and harbor-like seating area in this pondside landscape.

Swinging Benches

The pleasure of swinging is not just for kids at the playground. Relax to the soothing rhythm of a swinging bench with a loved one in the shade or under the stars.

1. A swinging bench is among the most romantic of vantage points. The rhythmic back and forth lulls and delights in this enchanting landscape. 2. Whenever you find a horizontal branch of an old oak tree, make sure to place a swinging bench there. Here, two different lengths of chain are secured to the leaning limb with a stone landing pad beneath. 3. An arbor is a roofed structure from which a swinging bench can hang. Cover it with climbing roses and surround it with activity in the swimming pool, and it will be well used.

Light and Lively

One senses owner-designer Marianne Zwahlen's personality everywhere in this unique Denver garden. The arbor with its retractable striped awning has a gypsy-caravan-like charm, but the dining table and chairs underneath bespeak a comforting solidity, and the teak grows more weathered and charming every year. Furniture in the garden is painted in bright colors and pastels that are echoed in the garden beds and container plantings. The refreshing informality makes one want to sit down, pour a glass of iced tea . . . and stay a while.

below • The slightly zany paint job on the garden house and bench lifts the spirits and keeps this garden from being too "pretty."

left · The striped canopy overhead provides the airiest of coverings for the patio dining table. From the protection of the seating area, one can enjoy the garden, whose blend of foliage colors and textures creates visual interest wherever the eye travels.

below · The artfully looping grapevine subtly yet playfully echoes the interlocking circle pattern of the patio. Rock-bordered flowerbeds, overflowing with classic cottage-garden plants such as alliums and blue bachelor's buttons, float like islands among the gravel walkways.

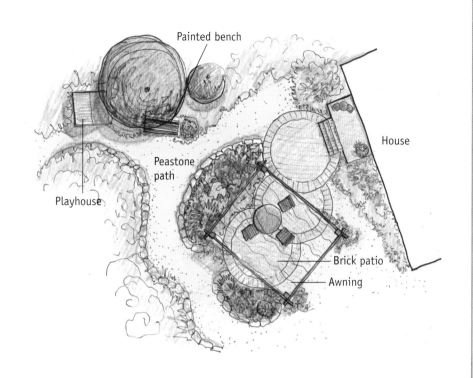

Painted bench

Playhouse

Peastone path

House

Brick patio

Awning

LOUNGING

Few things promise whole-hearted enjoyment of the outdoors as much as a hammock or lounge chair. Their only purpose is to promote lazing, snoozing, and daydreaming. Even the sight of an empty hammock seems to lower your blood pressure. It's worth it to spend a little extra for a good-quality hammock that won't flip and tangle, and take proper care of it in the off-season to extend its life. If you happen to have two perfectly spaced trees, you are lucky—but you can also make do with a post or wall, and some even come with their own frames.

right • Two building corners provide the perfect setting and support for hanging a hammock over a private deck.

below • Find two old trees about 15 ft. apart and you can string up a large rope hammock between them. Screw in your hangers about 5 ft. above the ground.

right • This inviting armchair and ottoman and accompanying loveseat on a sheltered patio are perfectly placed for the peaceful contemplation of an expansive view.

Give Your Old Furniture a Field Day

It's amazing what you can find at a dump or yard sale to repurpose for your outdoor spaces. A good sealant and coat of varnish can protect wood outdoors. Look for one that resists cracking or blistering and protects wood from harmful UV rays. If painting old wood, make sure to first treat it with a bleach solution for mildew or mold, then sand or roughen the surface, and apply a primer and then a finish coat. Every year, wash it thoroughly with warm water and dish detergent and it will last for years to come.

Lighting

Thoughtful outdoor lighting puts the frosting on the cake. It can highlight and enhance views of your garden from indoors at night, and it can also extend the hours during which you enjoy your outdoor spaces. You don't need to light the entire landscape; look for the particular features you wish to illuminate. Use lighting as a safety feature, making paths and entrances clearly visible at night, and make it easy for you and your guests to travel between outdoor living spaces and the house itself. Look for solar and alternative-powered options that will reduce your energy usage; in recent years, LEDs have improved greatly, now offering warmer light and dimming options that beautify the nighttime landscape.

Uplighting from either a can set into the ground or a moveable hooded element can spotlight a special tree or feature.

These hooded spot lights submersed in crushed stone illuminate the curvature of the sculpture. If the location poses a tripping hazard, substitute flush angled well lights. A portable candle lantern enlivens the scene.

A candlelit chandelier hangs from a long tree branch to bring ambience to this comfortable sitting area.

Night Lights

Lighting your property at night provides both physical safety and home security, but it can also transform a familiar landscape into a magical, mysteriously inviting place. While an overhead spotlight will adequately illuminate paths and entrances, lighting placed closer to ground level will perform the same function but cast fewer severe shadows and blind spots. Find light fixtures that blend with or complement the style of your home—perhaps echoing the pattern of an architectural feature such as a front door design or leaded-glass window.

4

5

1. Wherever there's a level change, the steps need to be well lit. Small fixtures can create soft highlights that guide you through the landscape, so that at each point one looks ahead to the next. 2. Sometimes the best fixtures are battery-powered. Here, a downlight shows the edge of the freestanding wall, while a tall lantern lights the cap. 3. Outdoor fixtures like this verdigris sconce can be situated not only to illuminate paths and steps, but also to cast a golden glow over a desired area, transforming it into a magically welcoming space by night. 4. This bollard is ornamental and functional, providing unobtrusive downlighting on two sides, illuminating two intersecting paths. 5. A hanging lantern set into grapevines casts beautiful leafy shadows.

A Complete Courtyard

This two-level outdoor space in an urban courtyard fulfills many functions in a small area. Sitting and entertaining, outdoor dining for children and adults, and storage space are all harmoniously integrated in this design. Continuity of materials—chiefly stained wood and brick—pulls it all together, while a planting palette of green, white, and soft yellow also makes the space feel coherent and not too "busy." Mature trees and a well-filled-in privacy hedge provide verdant walls of green.

below • Four distinct seating areas peacefully coexist in a remarkably small space without feeling a bit cluttered. The design accommodated a palm tree whose silvery, horizontally banded bark provides a contrasting accent. Attractive staircase lighting ensures that evening guests won't miss a step.

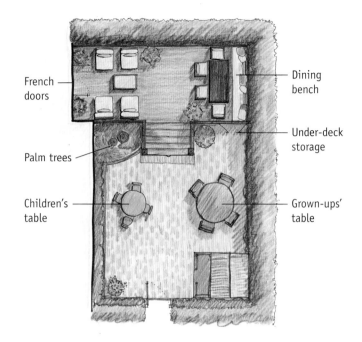

French doors

Dining bench

Palm trees

Under-deck storage

Children's table

Grown-ups' table

right • The placement of these comfortable chairs flanking the French doors invites people to move freely between indoor and outdoor living rooms. Although the furniture design is simple and unfussy, the hardware details of doorhandle and lighting fixtures convey a quiet elegance.

bottom left • The furniture perfectly matches the deck railings and floorboards, so that spaces with different functions are seamlessly connected. Potted plants soften the manmade edges and surfaces.

bottom right • Cupboards ingeniously concealed beneath the deck allow for storage of gardening tools and children's playthings.

CREDITS

p. i: © Mark Lohman, design: Eagleton Landscape

p. ii: © Susan Teare, design: John K. Szczepaniak, Landscape Architect

p. iv (left to right): © Susan Teare, design: AJ Miller Landscape Architecture; © Eric Roth; © Eric Roth, design: Lynda Sutton

p. v (left to right): © Mark Lohman, design: Janet Lohman Landscape Design; © Allan Mandell, design: Marina Wynton, Portland, OR; © Susan Teare, design: John K. Szczepaniak, Landscape Architect; © Allan Mandell, design: Tom Hobbs, Vancouver, BC

p. 2 (top, left to right): © Bluegreen|Jason Dewey, design: Bluegreen; © Allan Mandell, design: Cassandra and Brian Barrett, Dexter, OR; © Mark Lohman; © Eric Roth, design: Kate Adams

(bottom): © Allan Mandell, design: Joanne Fuller, Portland, OR, pebble mosaic: Jeff Bale, Portland, OR

p. 3: © Melissa Clark Photography, design: Melissa Clark, APLD

CHAPTER 1

p. 4: © Mark Lohman

p. 6: (top) © Brian Vanden Brink; (bottom) © Eric Roth, design: Gayle Mandel

p. 7: © Mark Lohman

p. 8: (top) © Brian Vanden Brink; (bottom) © Eric Roth, design: www.daherinteriordesign.com

p. 10-11: © Mark Lohman, design: Eagleton Landscape

p. 12: © Tria Giovan

p. 13: (top) © Brian Vanden Brink; (bottom) © Laurie Black, design: Lisa Port, APLD, Banyon Tree Design Studio

p. 14: (top) © Mark Lohman; (bottom) © Bluegreen|Jason Dewey, design: Bluegreen

p. 15: (top) © Banyon Tree Design Studio, design: Lisa Port, APLD, Banyon Tree Design Studio; (bottom) © Laurie Black, design: Lisa Port, APLD, Banyon Tree Design Studio

p. 16: (top) © Mark Lohman; (bottom) © Chipper Hatter, materials: Amcor

p. 17: © Susan Teare, design: JMMDS

p. 18: © Susan Teare, design: JMMDS

p. 19: (top left) © JMMDS; (top right) © Susan Teare, design: JMMDS; (bottom) © Susan Teare, design: JMMDS

CHAPTER 2

p. 20: © Susan Teare, design: John K. Szczepaniak, Landscape Architect

p. 22: (top) © Chipper Hatter, materials: Amcor; (bottom) © Chipper Hatter

p. 24: (top) © Eric Roth, design: Betsy Speert; (bottom) © Melissa Clark Photography, design: Melissa Clark, APLD

p. 25: (top) © Chip Callaway, design: Callaway & Associates, Chip Callaway; (bottom) © Broadleaf Landscape Architecture, design: Broadleaf Landscape Architecture

p. 26: © Susan Teare, design: AJ Miller Landscape Architecture

p. 27: © Susan Teare, design: AJ Miller Landscape Architecture

p. 28: (top) © Victoria Lister Carley, design: Victoria Lister Carley Landscape Architect; (bottom) © Banyon Tree Design Studio, design: Lisa Port, APLD, Banyon Tree Design Studio

p. 29: © Susan Teare, design: John K. Szczepaniak, Landscape Architect

p. 30: (top) © Mark Lohman; (bottom) © Laurie Black, design: Lisa Port, APLD, Banyon Tree Design Studio

p. 31 (top) © Mark Lohman; (bottom) © Mark Lohman

p. 32: © Mark Lohman

p. 33: © Susan Teare, design: JMMDS

p. 34: © AJ Miller Landscape Architecture, design: AJ Miller Landscape Architecture

p. 35: (top) © Eric Roth; (bottom) © Eric Roth, design: www.lombardidesign.com

p. 36: (top) © Brian Vanden Brink, design: Meyer "Farnsworth", Waldoboro, ME; (bottom) © Lee Anne White, design and construction: Red Rock Pools & Spas

p. 37: © Mark Lohman

p. 38: (top) © Roy Grogan, design: John K. Szczepaniak, Landscape Architect; (bottom) © Eric Roth, design: www.christinetuttle.com

p. 39: © Eric Roth

p. 40: (left) © Allan Mandell, design: Jack Hagenaars and Keith Webb, Victoria BC, Canada; (right) © Eric Roth

p. 41: © Brian Vanden Brink, design: Bernhardt and Priestley Architecture

p. 42: (top) © Susan Teare; (bottom) © Mark Lohman

p. 43: © Allan Mandell, design: Elaine and Justin Gammon, Victoria, BC

p. 44: (top) © Brian Vanden Brink; (bottom) © Eric Roth

p. 45: (top) © 2010 Arbonies King Vlock; ; (bottom) © Jim Fiora, design: Sandra Vlock of Arbonies King Vlock, Architects

p. 46: © Roy Grogan, design: John K. Szczepaniak, Landscape Architect

p. 47: (top) © Susan Teare, design: John K. Szczepaniak, Landscape Architect; (bottom) © Susan Teare, design: John K. Szczepaniak, Landscape Architect

p. 48: (left) © Jim Fiora, design: Sandra Vlock of Arbonies King Vlock, Architects; (right) © Brian Vanden Brink, design: Polhemus Savery DaSilva Architects Builders

p. 49: (top) © JMMDS, design: JMMDS; (bottom) © Eric Roth

CHAPTER 3

p. 50: © Eric Roth, design: www.foleyfiore.com

p. 52: (left) © Mark Lohman; (right) © Eric Roth, design: www.horstbuchanan.com

p. 53: © Tria Giovan

p. 54: © Mark Lohman

p. 55: (top) © Eric Roth; (bottom) © Kenneth Walpita of MGS Architecture, design: Magdalena Glen-Schieneman, AIA of MGS Architecture

p. 56: (top) © Jim Fiora, design: AKV Architects; (bottom) © Eric Roth, design: www.svdesign.com

p. 57: © Susan Teare, design: AJ Miller Landscape Architecture

p. 58: (top) © Eric Roth; (bottom) Mark Lohman

p. 59: (top) © Eric Roth, design: www.bkarch.com; (bottom) © AJ Miller Landscape Architecture, design: AJ Miller Landscape Architecture

p. 60: © Jim Fiora, design: Sandra Vlock of Arbonies King Vlock, Architects

p. 61: (top) © 2010 Arbonies King Vlock; (bottom) © 2010 Arbonies King Vlock, design: Sandra Vlock of Arbonies King Vlock, Architects

p. 62: (top) © Allan Mandell, design: Linda Ernst, Portland, OR; (bottom) © Victoria Lister Carley, design: Victoria Lister Carley Landscape Architect

p. 63: © Brian Vanden Brink, design: Ennead Architects

p. 64: © Susan Teare, design: John K. Szczepaniak, Landscape Architect

p. 65: (top) © Susan Teare, design: John K. Szczepaniak, Landscape Architect; (bottom) © JSZLA

p. 66: (top) © Chipper Hatter; (bottom) © Banyon Tree Design Studio, design: Lisa Port, APLD, Banyon Tree Design Studio

p. 67: (left) © Mark Lohman; (top right) © Chipper Hatter, materials: Georgia Masonry Supply; (bottom right) © Chipper Hatter

p. 68: (left) © Allan Mandell, design: Ron Wagner and Nani Waddoups, Portland, OR; (top right) © Eric Roth; (bottom right) © Brian Vanden Brink

p. 69: © Bill Sumner, design: JMMDS

p. 70: (top) © Victoria Lister Carley, design: Victoria Lister Carley Landscape Architect; (bottom) © Lee Anne White, design: Da Vida Pools, landscape design: Bill Roberts

p. 71: (top) © Lee Anne White, design: Kristina Kessel and David Thorne, David Thorne Landscape Architects; (bottom) © Mark Lohman, design: Janet Lohman Landscape Design

p. 72: (top) © Brian Vanden Brink; (bottom) © Todd Caverly

p. 73: (top left) © Brian Vanden Brink, design: Phi Home Designs; (bottom left) © Brian Vanden Brink; (right) © Brian Vanden Brink, design: South Mountain Company

p. 74: (left) © Eric Roth, design: Kate Adams; (top right) © Brian Vanden Brink; (bottom right) © Susan Teare, design: John K. Szczepaniak, Landscape Architect

p. 75: (top left) © Suzanne Albinson, design: Suzanne Albinson; (bottom left) © Todd Caverly; (top right) © Tria Giovan; (bottom right) © Todd Caverly

p. 148: © Laurie Black, design: Lisa Port, APLD, Banyon Tree Design Studio

p. 149: © Laurie Black, design: Lisa Port, APLD, Banyon Tree Design Studio

p. 150: (top) © Susan Teare, design: AJ Miller Landscape Architecture; (bottom) © Mark Lohman

p. 151: (top) © Mark Lohman; (bottom) © Broadleaf Landscape Architecture, design: Broadleaf Landscape Architecture

p. 152: (top) © Allan Mandell, design: Cassandra & Brian Barrett, Dexter, OR; (bottom) © Mark Lohman, design: Sally Kanin

p. 153: (top) © Susan Teare, design: Broadleaf Landscape Architecture ; (bottom) © Virginia Weiler, design: Nancy Spencer and Kevin Lindsey

p. 154: (top) © Brian Vanden Brink, design: Bernhardt and Priestley Architecture; (bottom) © Suzanne Albinson, design: Suzanne Albinson

p. 155: © Susan Teare, design: Broadleaf Landscape Architecture

p. 156: (top) © Broadleaf Landscape Architecture, design: Broadleaf Landscape Architecture; (bottom) © Suzanne Albinson, design: Suzanne Albinson

p. 157: (top) Marc Vassallo, courtesy of Kitchen Gardener, © The Taunton Press, Inc.; (bottom) © Eric Roth, design: http://katherinefield.com

p. 158: (top) © Bill Sumner, design: JMMDS; (bottom) © Bill Sumner, design: JMMDS

p. 159: © Bill Sumner, design: JMMDS

p. 160: (left) © Chipper Hatter, landscape architect: Jeffrey Carbo ASLA; (top right) © Chipper Hatter, landscape architect: Jeffrey Carbo ASLA; (bottom right) © Allan Mandell, design: Stacie Crooks, Seattle, WA

p. 161: © Brian Vanden Brink, design: Hutker Architects

p. 162: © Lee Anne White, design: Four Dimensions Landscape Co.

p. 163: © Lee Anne White, design: Four Dimensions Landscape Co.

p. 164: (top) © Erica Bowman, design: Andromeda Designs; (bottom) © Chip Callaway, design: Callaway and Associates, Chip Callaway

p. 165: © Virginia Weiler, design: Nancy Spencer and Kevin Lindsey

p. 166: (top) © Allan Mandell, design: Tom Hobbs, Vancouver, BC; (bottom) © Allan Mandell, design: Marina Wynton, Portland, OR

p. 167: © Bluegreen|Jason Dewey, design: Bluegreen

p. 168: (left) © Michael Thilgen, design: Four Dimensions Landscape Co.; (right) © Mark Lohman

p. 169: © Mark Lohman, design: Eagleton Landscape

p. 170: (left) © Jim Fiora, design: Sandra Vlock of Arbonies King Vlock, Architects; (right) © Susan Teare, design: AJ Miller Landscape Architecture

p. 171: © Susan Teare, design: AJ Miller Landscape Architecture

p. 172: (left) © Mark Lohman; (right) © Susan Teare, design: AJ Miller Landscape Architecture

p. 173: (top left) © Allan Mandell, design: Jim Bishop, San Diego, CA; (bottom left) © Banyon Tree Design Studio, design: Lisa Port, APLD, Banyon Tree Design Studio; (right) © Mark Lohman, design: Janet Lohman Landscape Design

p. 174: (top) © Suzanne Albinson, design: Suzanne Albinson; (bottom) Jennifer Bartley, courtesy of Fine Gardening, © The Taunton Press, Inc.

p. 175: (top) © Eric Roth; (bottom) David Cavagnaro, courtesy of Fine Gardening, © The Taunton Press, Inc.

p. 176: (left) © Mark Lohman, design: Marilee Kuhlmann; (right) © Mark Lohman, design: Marilee Kuhlmann

p. 177: © Mark Lohman, design: Marilee Kuhlmann

p. 178: (left) © Marilee Kuhlmann, design: Comfort Zones Garden Design; (right) © Allan Mandell, design: Audrey and John Burrows, Calgary, AB

p. 179: (top) © Erica Bowman; (bottom) © Eric Roth, design: Lynda Sutton

CHAPTER 7

p. 180: Allan Mandell, design: Rob Bond, Victoria BC

p. 182: (top) © Chipper Hatter, design: Mesa Design, landscape architects: Jeff Carbo; (bottom) ©

Laurie Black, design: Lisa Port, APLD, Banyon Tree Design Studio

p. 183: © Susan Teare, design: AJ Miller Landscape Architecture

p. 184: (top) © Bluegreen|Jason Dewey, design: Bluegreen; (bottom) © Mark Lohman, design: Sally Kanin

p. 185: © Brian Vanden Brink, design: Dominic Mercadante, Architect

p. 186: (left) © Mark Lohman; (top right) © Mark Lohman; (bottom right) © Susan Teare, design: JMMDS

p. 187: (left) © Allan Mandell, design: Joanne Fuller, Portland, OR, glass art by Barbara Sanderson, Mukilteo, WA; (right) © Chipper Hatter, landscape architect: Jeffrey Carbo ASLA

p. 188: (left) © Lee Anne White, design: Bobby Saul; (top right) © JMMDS, design: JMMDS; (bottom right) © Bluegreen|Jason Dewey, design: Bluegreen

p. 189: © Ken Gutmaker, design: Patricia St. John, APLD

p. 190: (left) © Susan Teare, design: Broadleaf Landscape Architecture; (right) © Susan Teare, design: John K. Szczepaniak, Landscape Architect

p. 191: (top) © Susan Teare, design: AJ Miller Landscape Architecture; (bottom) © Allan Mandell, design: Steelman-Sams, Eugene, OR

p. 192: (left) © Susan Teare, design: Broadleaf Landscape Architecture ; (right) © Susan Teare, design: Broadleaf Landscape Architecture

p. 193: (top) © Eric Roth, design: John Platt; (bottom) © Brian Vanden Brink, architects: Group 3, builder: Hankin Group

p. 194: (top) © Bluegreen|Jason Dewey, design: Bluegreen; (bottom) © Chipper Hatter, materials: Amcor

p. 195: © Ken Gutmaker, design: Patricia St. John, APLD

p. 196: © Susan Teare, design: JMMDS

p. 197: (top) © Susan Teare, design: JMMDS; (bottom) © Susan Teare, design: JMMDS

p. 198: (top) © Lee Anne White, design and construction: Red Rock Pools and Spas; (bottom) Chipper Hatter, materials: Amcor

p. 199: (top) Charles Miller, courtesy of Fine Homebuilding, © The Taunton Press, Inc.; (bottom) © Chipper Hatter

p. 200: (left) © Allan Mandell, design: Mark and Mouse Scharfenager, Denver, CO; (top right) © Tria Giovan; (bottom right) © Laurie Black, design: Lisa Port, APLD, Banyon Tree Design Studio

p. 201: (top) © Allan Mandell, design: Joanne Fuller, Portland, OR; (bottom) © Eric Roth

p. 202: (left) © Susan Teare, design: JMMDS; (top right) © Brian Vanden Brink, design: Weatherend Estate Furniture; (bottom right) © Todd Caverly, design: Weatherend Estate Furniture, Rockland, ME

p. 203: (left) © Mark Lohman; (top right) © Mark Lohman; (bottom right) © Mark Lohman

p. 204: (left) © Mark Lohman, design: Marianne Zwahlen; (right) © Mark Lohman, design: Marianne Zwahlen

p. 205: © Mark Lohman, design: Marianne Zwahlen

p. 206: (top) © Brian Vanden Brink; (bottom) © Brian Vanden Brink

p. 207: (top) © Brian Vanden Brink, design: Peter Rose + Partners, Stowe, VT; (bottom) © Allan Mandell, design: Audrey and John Burrows, Calgary, AB

p. 208: (top) © Lee Anne White, design: Hillary Curtis and David Thorne, David Thorne Landscape Architects; (bottom) © Susan Teare, design: AJ Miller, Landscape Architects

p. 209: © Mark Lohman

p. 210: (left) © Susan Teare, design: AJ Miller Landscape Architecture; (top right) © Susan Teare, design: AJ Miller Landscape Architecture; (bottom right) © Susan Teare, design: AJ Miller Landscape Architecture

p. 211: (left) © Susan Teare, design: John K. Szczepaniak, Landscape Architect; (right) © Susan Teare, design: Broadleaf Landscape Architecture

p. 212: © Mark Lohman

p. 213: (top) © Mark Lohman; (bottom left) © Mark Lohman; (bottom right) © Mark Lohman

INDEX

A

Annuals, 168–69
Arbors, 60–61, 185, 203, 204
Artworks. *See* Sculpture

B

Backyards
contemporary, 37
design of, 36
as gathering spaces, 38–39
as getaways, 40–41
as play spaces, 42–43
transforming, examples of,
18–20, 60–61
Benches, 202–3
Birdhouses, 105, 186
Bridges, 132–33
Bugs, 179

C

Chlorine, alternatives to, 70
Climbing vines, 100–101, 154–55
Cold frames, 178
Courtyards, urban, 39, 212–13

D

Decks, 58
examples of, 10–11, 60–61
materials for, 59
as open-air rooms, 52
railings, 58, 106–7
Design
backyards, 36 (*see also*
Backyards)
basic layouts, 23
beginning steps, 6
drawing a plan, 9
driveways and garages, 44–47
front yards, 24 (*see also* Front
yards)
plantings, 136–39 (*see also*
Plantings)
side yards, 32–35, 196–97
wish list, creating, 16–17
your house and, 12
your property and, 8, 10
your style and, 14
Details. *See* Focal points
Driveways, 44–47, 48–49

E

Edging, 108
examples of, 108, 109, 112
materials and techniques for,
110–11
Edible plants, 25, 174–77
Enclosures, 82
edging, 108–12
gateways, 82, 104–5, 185
hedges, 102–3
railings, 106–7
walls (*see* Walls)

F

Fences, 98
birdhouse posts, 105
examples of, 64–65, 83, 98–99
gateways, 82, 104–5, 185
plants climbing on, 100–101
Fire
as focal point, 194–99
garden, 196–97
outdoor kitchens, 199
Firebowls, 195
Firepits, 194, 196–97
Fireplaces, 198
Flooring, moisture issues and, 54
Focal points, 184
details, delighting in, 182–83
dynamic, 186–87
fire, 194–99
framing effects, 184–85
furniture (*see* Furniture)
lighting, 182–83, 208–11
sculpture, 182, 184, 187
stone, 188–89
water, 27, 190–93
Formal gardens, 26–27, 175
Fountains, 27, 190–91
Framing effects, 184–85
Front yards
design of, 24
edible, 25
enclosed, 30
formal, 26–27
romantic, 31
stepped, 28–29
Furniture
benches, 202
as focal point, 200–201
in a garden, 204–5
lounging, 206–7
repurposing used, 207
swinging benches, 203

G

Garages, 44, 46–47
Gardens. *See* Plantings
Gateways, 82, 104–5, 185
Grasses, 160–61
Greenhouses, 178–79
Green ideas. *See* Sustainability
and the environment
Green roofs, 166–67
Grills, 54–55, 199
Ground covers, 164–65

H

Hammocks, 206
Handrails, 106–7
Hedges, 102–3
Hot tubs, 72

K

Kitchens, outdoor, 199

L

Landscapes
East meets West in, 78–79
engaging with nature through,
3
personal style and, 14–15,
204–5
Lawns, 68–69
Lighting
as focal point, 182–83, 208–9
nighttime, 210–11
Lounge chairs, 207

M

Modern homesteading, 174, 178

N

Night lights, 210–11

O

Open-air rooms, 52–53
decks, 58–61
examples of, 6, 7, 16, 22, 53,
78–79, 83
hot tubs and spas, 72
lawns, 68–69
outdoor showers, 73
patios, 62–67
pools, 70–71
porches, 54–57
shade structures, 76–77
sheds and outbuildings, 74–75
Outbuildings, 41. *See also* Sheds
Outdoor kitchens, 199
Outdoor showers, 73

P

Pathways, 114–15
bridges, 132–33
formal, 116–17
informal, 122–23
joining contrasting styles of,
120–21
materials for, 126–27
paving, examples of, 14, 46–49
semiformal, 118–19
side yards and, 32–35
soft, 124–25
steps and stairs (*see* Steps and
stairs)
Patios, 62
examples of, 24
fire garden on, 196–97
as open-air rooms, 52, 64–65
paving options for, 62–63,
66–67
Paving strips, 48–49
Perennials, 156–57
Pergolas, 34, 60–61, 76–77
Pest control, 179
Plantings
annuals, 168–69
backyard transformation and,
19
bed layouts, 138–39
character of your house and,
12–13, 15
climbing vines, 100–101,
154–55

in containers, 170–73, 175
a driveway and, 45
edible, 25, 174–77
erosion control, 8
in front yards, 24–26
grasses, 160–61
greenhouses, 178–79
green roofs, 166–67
ground covers, 164–65
hedges, 102–3
lawns and, 69
linked gardens, themed
 landscape as, 158–59
on linked terraces, 94–95
as natural habitat, 157
perennials, 156–57
pest control in the garden, 179
rain gardens, 140–41
schemes for, 136–37
shrubs, 152–53
trees (see Trees)
xeriscaping, 162–63
Play spaces, 42–43
Pools, 70–71, 192–93
Porches, 54
 covered, 33
 as open-air rooms, 52, 54–55
 screened, 56–57
Potted plants, 170–73, 175
Privacy, 22, 39, 145–47

R

Railings, 58, 106–7
Rain gardens, 140–41
Retaining walls, 16

S

Screened frames, 52
Screened porches, 56–57
Sculpture, 182, 184, 187, 208
Sczcepaniak, John, 46, 64
Shade structures, 76–77
Sheds, 52, 74–75
Showers, outdoor, 73
Shrubs
 flowering, 153
 foliage and color from, 152
Side yards, 32–35, 196–97
Soil, 10
Spaces, 22
 backyards (see Backyards)
 driveways and garages, 44–47
 enclosed, 82 (see also
  Enclosures)
 front yards (see Front yards)

layout of, 23
side yards, 32–35
See also Design
Spas, 72
Steps and stairs, 128
 front yard, 28–29
 garden, 129
 landings, 130–31
 lighting for, 211
 railings, 106–7
Stone
 edging, 108, 110
 as a focal point, 188–89
 pathways, 14, 46–47, 114,
  118–23, 126–27
 paving strips, 48–49
 steps, 128–31
 terraces, 64–67
 walls, 82, 85, 86–87
Sustainability and the
 environment
 chlorine alternatives, 70
 decking materials, 59
 furniture, repurposing used,
  207
 green roofs, 166–67
 green walls, 88–89
 natural habitat in the garden,
  157
 rain gardens, 140–41
Swimming pools, 70–71, 192–93
Swinging benches, 203

T

Terraces, linked, 94–95. See also
 Patios
Trees, 142
 colors provided by, 150–51
 evergreens, 142, 146
 mature, 143
 privacy provided by, 145,
  146–47
 as structure, 144
 tropical, 15, 148–49
Tropical retreat, 15, 148–49

W

Walls, 84
 of an urban courtyard, 39
 concrete, 84–85
 connecting terraces, 94–95
 fences, 98–101
 green, 88–89
 materials for, 96–97
 retaining, 16

seating, 92–93
stone, 82, 85, 86–87
tiled, 90–91
Water
 as focal point, 27, 190–93
 fountains, 27, 190–91
 long channel of, 187
 swimming pools, 70–71,
  192–93
Wind, 10
Wind chimes, 186, 187

X

Xeriscaping, 162–63